HAIR ON FIRE:

A HEARTWARMING & HUMOROUS CHRISTMAS MEMOIR

LARADA HORNER-MILLER

To buy books in quantity for corporate use or incentives, call (505) 323-798 or e-mail larada@LaradasBooks.com

ISBN-13: 978-0-9966144-8-1 (Horner Publishing Company)

In order to maintain anonymity, I have changed the name of an individual.

Cover by: 100Covers.com

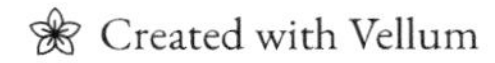

CONTENTS

ACKNOWLEDGMENTS

Publishing a book is a daunting task. I have a support team that makes it happen repeatedly. Here's my team:

- My editor, Parisa Zolfaghari, from www.reedsy.com who I have worked with on the last four books. I thoroughly enjoy our editorial exchange and Parisa's lighthearted sense of humor.
- The East Mountain Group of Cody, Marty and Maia have continued on this writing path with me —Cody and Marty for eight glorious years.
- My Advance Reader Team who provided insight and helpful comments tightening up the manuscript.

You are the best!

I dedicate this book to

- My mom and dad, who made all my Christmases memorable
- The Branson Community Church, which grounded me in my love for Christ and Christmas
- My Sunday school teacher who took care of my hair on fire
- My husband, Lin, who makes all our Christmases enjoyable

"Christmas is a season not only of rejoicing but of reflection."

—*Winston Churchill*

INTRODUCTION

Christmas—just this one word conjures up so many images and memories: a snow-covered pasture, pristine and shiny white; caroling on a cold winter night, hands and feet numb, yet oblivious to it because of the joy and laughter; and a boisterous family gathering to prepare for Santa Claus.

In December 2021, my husband, Lin, and I traveled to Italy and Spain, and saw the decorations and celebrations they had prepared for their own traditional Christmas. People displayed Nativity sets, creches, freely. Santa Claus appeared everywhere. Red, white, and green decorations covered windows and counters in stores. People smiled when I wished them "Merry Christmas" in their native language. My joy around Christmas only grew as I realized how big our world is, yet how much we are alike!

As we traveled around the two countries, surrounded by festive white lights and the locals' holiday cheer, I was inspired. The moment we came home, I began to compile my favorite memories and thoughts about this holy day. That's how this book came to be. It spans from my rural country childhood to my adult life in a variety of cities and countries, yet each place had its joyous memories.

What does hair on fire have to do with Christmas? It's one of the many memorable childhood Christmases I've had in my life, and it's a memory that still makes me chuckle. I was five or six years old and an angel in our annual church Christmas program. I had never had a part in the program before to this size, so I felt privileged and excited to be included. Each angel carried a candle, and that's where the mishap took place. Afterward, we went on as if nothing happened. I had forgotten this incident for many years, then in writing my first book, *This Tumbleweed Landed,* I wrote a poem about the Branson church, and up came the memory! It still makes me laugh with the outcome—resolved effortlessly and matter-of-factly. No one was hurt, no blood spilled, and things were handled quickly. The whole episode embodies a rancher's attitude toward life.

Traveling around in 2021, making new memories, served to bring these other core memories to the forefront. None are better than the other, but I do have my favorites!

Several of the pieces in here are stories and poetry I've written over the years in my weekly blog. A few of them were included in my chapbook, *A Country Christmas,* which received positive reviews. A chapbook is a short booklet of 20-40 pages. I realized at that point my stories had universal interest. *A Country Christmas* was mostly made up of my childhood memories. As an adult, I moved to other towns and cities and obtained other precious memories and added traditions. My world travel last year enlarged my Christmas memories even more, and I decided it was time for a new book to be born.

Much of this book is original, made up of a mix of narrative and poetry, but there are a few poems that appeared in previous books. I love storytelling, and the differences in how the narrative and poems convey the feelings, thoughts, and impact of the memory, and I love the variety of it all.

In a couple of the readings, I pondered those familiar two people I heard about all my life who were present that Christmas day so long ago: Mary and Joseph. I wrote about walking beside this couple to see what the journey to Bethlehem felt like.

As you read my memories, I hope it sparks joyful remembrances for you—let your child revel in the holiday of all holidays. The readings stand alone, so you can read this book from cover to cover or select a topic that speaks to you!

Are you ready to welcome the Holy Family into your home tonight? You may have a Nativity set up in your home, but are you ready to offer Mary and Joseph a place in your heart to birth the Christ child? I hope you do!

Merry Christmas!

CHAPTER ONE

MARY AND JOSEPH: WALK WITH THEM!

On this day, many years ago, pregnant Mary and Joseph traveled to Bethlehem because of Caesar Augustus's decree. It was only ninety-three miles, about a two and a half hour trip in a car, but remember, Mary rode a donkey. Joseph walked. I wondered what it would be like walking with them and imagined myself joining this couple and their unusual life-changing experience!

It had to be a struggle for Mary—and for Joseph as he watched her. A struggle for both. I watched them—Mary absorbed in her pregnancy and this ordeal, and Joseph stressed as he watched Mary.

Their baby was due at any time. In fact, Mary had warned him she felt the event they had been waiting for was almost here!

The donkey's slow pace rocks Mary into a lulled state. Her head bobs, but she is safe because Joseph keeps his hand on her leg to keep her from falling off. The silence surrounds them. I smell the strong pungent donkey odor that lingers in the air. He brays, asking to stop, so we do. I respect their privacy and keep my distance, but I marvel as Joseph cares for her.

With Joseph's help, Mary rolls off the donkey and discreetly relieves herself in the bushes. Joseph provides a small drink for the tired donkey and a bit of hay. He also quenches his and Mary's thirst, and they share a piece of bread to stay them. I grab my canteen and drink with them. My stomach growls as I forgot to bring any food for this journey. They hear the ominous rumble and share their meager snack with me.

As they negotiate getting Mary back up on the donkey, they laugh at the absurdity of their trip and her awkward size. And once again, they continue toward Bethlehem, resuming the rhythm of the donkey's gait. Watching their total acceptance of this needless trip, I want to help, but it's my job to just be there with them, a silent witness!

That beautiful part of the day comes—the link between darkness and light. This makes the travel much more treacherous. Joesph stumbles often, catching himself. He can't fall; he must make sure Mary's safe on their donkey. A couple times, I brace Joseph so he can keep going. I have to assist him because of the dark, because of the mission, because of the precious cargo he needs to protect.

Darkness comes, and a beautiful canopy of stars twinkle above us. One predominant star shines brighter and brighter, almost like it is guiding them to their destination. Then Mary's scream scares Joseph and me, and he knows the time is approaching too fast—way too fast. But she settles back into the rhythm of the road, and he knows she hides any discomfort from him, to protect him.

We haven't arrived yet in crowded Bethlehem. Because of their slow travel, we will arrive late in the evening, and they'll have a new problem: none of the inns will have room. But right now we are working our way to Bethlehem, anticipating what's ahead.

CHAPTER TWO

ADVENT: WHY ANTICIPATE CHRISTMAS?

Yes, it's only one day a year, but celebrating the whole season leading up to that day fulfills me as an adult—and as an eternal child.

My memories bolster me as I grow older. Each time, a specific event comes up, I rush for my computer to capture the thought and the feeling. I hope that enchantment never dies.

As an Episcopalian Christian, I take part in the season before Christmas, Advent. Surprisingly, I have never written about Advent, the weeks leading up to Christmas.

When I first became familiar with this season, I jumped in full force. Every year, I put out the Advent wreath. It held four candles—mine were purple—in a circle with a white one in the middle, the Christ candle.

In the morning before work, I lit first one candle the first week, then two, then three, and then four for the four weeks of Advent and read a corresponding prayer. When Christmas Eve came, I was supposed to light the white one in the middle, but often I forgot because of the busyness of the day. Still, I enjoyed the anticipatory energy this tradition gave me.

Then, for many years, I drifted away from this observance. I divorced my ex-husband and began a sad seven years of my life, basically turning my back on God.

After twenty more years of being angry at God for my divorce and the loss of my adopted child, I returned to my God, cautiously searching for a church. Advent had come and gone for so many years, I felt no connection to it anymore.

Every year around Thanksgiving, a faint remembrance of Advent swept over me, but my anger and pain won out. Then I found my present church, Hope in the Desert Episcopal Church, and a Higher Power I could work with through my recovery programs. Advent began to seep back into my life ever so slowly. The familiar quiet celebration of past years won out as I rediscovered the joy of Advent and the anticipation of Christmas anew. What I enjoyed the most was the focused anticipation of the birth of Christ, again, this year, not 2,000 years ago, but this year!

Two years ago, a friend from recovery asked if I wanted to do a phone group Advent study of Father Richard Rohr's book, *Preparing for Christmas: Daily Meditations for Advent*. What an inspiring experience that was. In this short book,

Father Rohr shares daily Scripture readings, a short commentary, and then a reflection question that helped me interact deeply with the theme of the day. I loved the focus on this instead of the commercialism in our world!

So last year, I reread the Rohr book by myself and once again enjoyed the anticipation of the birth of Christ.

I haven't done the Advent wreath recently, but maybe next year!

If you've never done it, now might be the time to give it a whirl.

CHAPTER
THREE
CHRISTMAS IS HERE!

The gifts are wrapped; cards and packages sent; the baking is done. Now is a lull. I like this time before the rush of the actual holiday.

The child in me remembers all those great Christmases and the anticipation. It was the anticipation that grabbed me

—waiting, waiting, waiting! And wondering if my dream would come true!

Traditions resounded in my childhood home: church program, program at school, and one of my favorites was shopping from the catalogs for months before Christmas.

Montgomery Ward—we called it Monkey Ward. I couldn't wait for the thick catalog to arrive. I would dog-ear the pages of what stuck out to me, revisiting that magical volume often. Then I would wait, wondering if I would get what I wanted.

Did you always get what you wanted? I didn't. Looking back, I now see I savor the anticipation as an adult, but I focused on the gifts as a child.

As an adult, I added more traditions and memories like the Advent observance and Christmas Eve Midnight Mass. I have learned: the gifts matter, yes, but the magic of the season lived on, no matter what gift I received.

CHAPTER

FOUR

WHEN DO YOU PUT UP YOUR CHRISTMAS TREE?

Many families have traditions that dictate when to put up the Christmas tree. Is earlier better? Right after Thanksgiving? How about Christmas Eve? Early December? When do you do it?

As a child, we put up our live piñon pine tree we'd cut down from our ranch around December 10th. As a family, we hunted for deer in October, walking the canyons and eyeing any future Christmas tree—big for me, my brother, and my dad; small for my mom—and scoping them out.

As an adult, any time I came home for Thanksgiving, we would cut down trees the weekend after Thanksgiving. Those trees stayed fresh to the touch until well after New Year's Day—no dry needles falling on the floor. I love live, fresh trees! We also cut fresh cedar boughs to spread around our houses. What a delicious smell that is, too!

So, I decided the earlier I put it up, the better! I usually put up my tree in the first week of December. That gives me more time to enjoy it and all the decorations after all the work of decorating.

For several years I spent Thanksgiving away from home, so no fresh, live piñon pine trees from our ranch. I bought "Live Trees" from lots in Albuquerque, New Mexico. It shocked me how dry they were—dried-up needles and no smell at all! To my horror, I found out the tree lots had bought trees cut down months before and from places far north of us.

Still, after my purchase, I hung the lights and marveled at the glow when I lit them. After completing my decoration routine, I'd sit back and admire my creation. Then one year, a week or two after lighting the tree, I smelled something hot near the tree and saw the electrical connection had a burnt spot and needles had fried!

After that near disaster, I realized I couldn't put up a near-dead tree and be safe for a month, like usual.

That forced us to buy an artificial tree! I returned to putting the artificial tree up the first week of December and that has been my habit ever since! I miss the smell of a piñon pine and the fun of cutting down a tree off our family ranch, but we've decided artificial is the way to go for now.

When do you put up your tree? Artificial or live?

CHAPTER FIVE

CHRISTMAS CAROLING

"Silent night."

"Joy to the World!" I love to sing Christmas carols. As a child, we sang those precious songs at church and school. At home, we sang along with the singers on the Lawrence Welk Christmas show, and there used to be so many Christmas specials—Andy Williams and Perry Como. I loved the bouncing ball on the Mitch Miller sing-along show. And of course, we watched "The Ed Sullivan Show" weekly and loved his Christmas special. I never grew tired of them.

One year when I was in high school, Margie Miller, one of our multi-talented teachers, taught us the first verse of "O Come All Ye Faithful" in Latin. It sounded so similar to the Spanish many of my friends spoke. Growing up in our small community of Branson, Colorado, I heard Spanish often. We started Spanish classes in fourth grade with Mrs. Gonzales, so I had an early introduction to learning this language.

The sound of this familiar Christmas hymn mesmerized me. Today, sixty-plus years later, I can still sing those Latin words to that wonderful old song.

In our small rural community during the 50s, 60s and 70s, I grew up at a time when church and state were not separate. We celebrated Christmas at school. During my high school years, we drove around Branson, Colorado on the back of a hay truck, singing Christmas carols for the community. At some point in the evening, someone always served hot chocolate and cookies to us chilly carolers.

Yes, it was cold on the back of that flatbed truck. We dressed warmly in layers of sweaters and heavy winter coats. A bright scarf and hand-knitted hat kept my head and neck warm. Mittens kept my fingers toasty, and snow boots donned my feet. I have the worst time keeping my feet warm, so I remember cold feet no matter what I had on my feet.

Even though I hate being cold, driving around on that hay truck became my favorite caroling experience.

We knew everyone in town, so it was exciting to see our friends' and neighbors' delight when we drove up to their houses. Most of the audience was elderly, and their eyes shone with joy as they heard all the songs they loved. Often, they joined in the singing.

The camaraderie we experienced singing those familiar songs welded us together. Our group was a tight-knit group anyway, but this shared experience of serving our community tightened the knot.

After about an hour of singing, we would go back to the school for our annual high school Christmas party. The main focus of the party was dancing—country and western dancing.

I have so many precious Christmas memories in that small town and school, but caroling around town, seeing the joy we spread, and dancing after, continuing that joy, is the one that rings strong and bright.

LYRICS TO THE FIRST VERSE "O COME ALL YE FAITHFUL":

O come, all ye faithful,
Joyful and triumphant!
O come ye, O come ye to Bethlehem;
Come and behold him
Born the King of angels:

Refrain
O come, let us adore Him,
O come, let us adore Him,
O come, let us adore Him,
Christ the Lord.

~

LATIN LYRICS TO THE FIRST VERSE ("ADESTE FIDELES"):

Adeste Fideles
Laeti triumphantes
Venite, venite in Bethlehem

Natum videte
Regem Angelorum

Refrain
Venite adoremus,
Venite adoremus,
Venite adoremus,
Dominum[1]

---

1. https://www.liveabout.com/adeste-fideles-english-and-latin-lyrics-2701295

CHAPTER
SIX
BRANSON COMMUNITY CHURCH

The Branson Community Church,
small and quaint.

People that touched my life
Maynard Bowen,
Walt Graham,
Ministers of God, who took their time for me.

Faithful attendees
The Loudens

The Gilstraps
The Smiths
The Warners
The Cummins
Mabel Survant
Mrs. Jamieson

The community of people
I saw each week,
Faithful
Friendly and
Influential in my early Christian training.

Sunday School teachers
and family friends who let me sit with them,
singing my songs out loud
even when I couldn't even read.
Beautiful old hymns and singing.

They loved me, taught me,
and encouraged me.
A safe place to be on Sunday morning,
and a nice place to meet God.

Each Sunday, I felt anchored
In love, looking at familiar faces,
In faith, as I watched Christianity in
Action
In my church home, so nurtured
And nourished in my spiritual life.

Youth group on Sunday night
games and talking about God

Youth group picnics and campouts at the
Gilstraps
and the annual Christmas programs.[1]

And every year, a Christmas program!

---

1. Adapted From: Larada Horner-Miller, *This Tumbleweed Landed* (2014): 31.

CHAPTER SEVEN

MY HAIR ON FIRE DOESN'T FIT WITH CHRISTMAS

As a child, the Branson Community Church played a huge part in my life. It's the people who loved and nurtured me whom I associate with in that quaint little church.

Each December, the Christmas program at the church was one of the big social events of the season for our small ranching community. It was a major part of our holiday festivities, and everyone in town who went to that church anticipated it. We put on pageants, songs, and plays.

Because of the cold wintry season, much of our social life stopped, so each time we gathered, it seemed so special and needed.

For one of the productions, I was an angel—I felt heavenly for sure. Being an angel can be dangerous! Here's what happened—safety wasn't the focus back in the 50s.

My Hair on Fire

Anticipation filled my heart.
We had practiced our Christmas pageant
several times,
Rehearsed and rehearsed.
I felt it was a winner.

I was young—maybe five or six.
I had a minor part, but it loomed large in my heart.
I was an angel, one of several.

Yet I felt special!
I loved my white gown (cut from a sheet),
my wings (cut from white paper)
and halo (a golden contraption that hovered over my head),
and my candle I carried (in my hands, no holder).
Teacher promised we would light it that night
But not during our practice.

Our teacher warned us each rehearsal:
the candles will be lit,
allow enough space between you and the angel
ahead of you!

When the big night came for our Christmas pageant, I dressed.
Mom curled my shoulder-length strawberry blonde hair.
It hung down to my shoulders in soft curls.
Before donning my halo, she sprayed an aura of her hair spray
which surprised me! She had never done that before!

Mom and Dad took me and my brother to our little country church.
I waved goodbye to them
and joined the others downstairs.

Excitement filled the air.
The teacher had Mary and Joseph lead the processional.
Next, the three shepherds fell in behind the holy couple.
The group of angels lined up after them—my turn!

The teacher passed out the candles, unlit.
It was time.

I stepped in line with a schoolmate behind me.
Soon the teacher came by and lit our candles,
whispering her warnings once again!

She had placed a paper shield around the candle
to protect our hands from the dripping wax!
Oh, there was so much to watch with a lit candle!

Up the stairs we went,

and the pageant proceeded as normal.

Then, for some reason, the angel group crowded together
instead of spacing out like our teacher suggested.
It was our time and the angel bunching continued.
Suddenly someone screamed, "Your hair is on fire!"

Quickly my teacher rushed over with a rolled paper
and whacked me on the head,
putting out the fire.

This haphazard event left me with singed hair,
and the burnt smell lingered.
Yes, it was a memorable Christmas,
and the pageant went on!

Our teachers served refreshments
Afterwards downstairs.
No one mentioned my hair
Or the fire!

SCRIPTURE – MATTHEW 1:23

Matthew 1:23 *"Behold, the virgin shall conceive and bear a son, and they shall call his name Immanuel" (which means, God with us).*

CHAPTER EIGHT

WHAT ARE YOUR CHRISTMAS TRADITIONS?

In my country childhood, we had many Christmas traditions: the fun and adventure of cutting down a tree from our ranch, hilarious Christmas programs at the church and school, and fun-filled Christmas caroling around our small town. Our family dominated this holiday's focus.

My dad's parents lived just across town, so most of my childhood Christmas Eves were spent at their house.

Christmas at the Horners'

IT WAS A BIG AFFAIR,
especially when Granddad got all
sixteen grandchildren together.
That meant a holiday house full.

EACH YEAR, my Christmas outfit was always special.
One year
a white dress with a gathered skirt,
trimmed in red,
made by Mom.

GRANDMA, decked out in her festive apron,
worried over the meal.
She made the best mashed potatoes,
smothered in butter.
Granddad's job came after dinner.

THE TABLE WAS SET on the porch so
we could all fit,
a long line of smiles and laughter.

FOR THOSE OF us who knew the tradition,

anticipation set in.
We tried to hurry the process,
with no success.

FINALLY, after a leisurely cup of coffee and a cigarette,
Granddad would disappear to the front door.

HIS SHOUT RANG through the whole house!
It had begun.

"I JUST SAW Santa Claus fly over. Come quick."

We'd race to the front door,
and
he would race to the back door.

"No, no, he's out here now. Come this way."

We'd race to the back door.
This would go on for
what seemed like eternity,
and I never did see Santa, a reindeer,
or his sleigh.
I was always a second too late!

But this also meant that it was time
to open our gifts that had mysteriously spilled out from
under the Christmas tree.

A traditional Christmas with the Horners meant
cousins,
aunts and uncles,
sometimes great aunts
from Tulsa, Oklahoma,
good food,
lots of laughter,
and
traditions that filled my heart with joy and
family connection![1]

. . .

WHAT WAS your favorite Christmas tradition?

---

1. Larada Horner-Miller, *This Tumbleweed Landed* (2014): 67-68.

CHAPTER
NINE
DEAR SANTA: YOU BROKE MY HEART

As I revisited Christmas once again in my mind, I reached back and remembered an incident etched in my memory, so I decided to write to dear old Saint Nick and question his practice one specific year so long ago.

Dear Santa,

I'm writing you an early pre-letter this year out of necessity.

Last year I asked for a desk, and I was so very specific. I saw it in the current Christmas catalog from Sears + Roebuck. Yes, I saw it was more than you usually spend on me, but I'm getting older, so I thought the price change matched my growing age.

Oh, what a desk! It's a roll top with two drawers on each side and little cubbyholes under the top for my many pens and pencils and favorite notes. I could just see myself sitting in front of it, doing my homework. When I finished, I could roll down the top. No mess, no papers cluttering my room!

I sent off my letter to you with a specific description and referenced the catalog number so you couldn't make a mistake. I knew you shopped there, too!

I started getting concerned when Mom and I talked one night after I sent off my letter. She brought up my request. How she knew about it was puzzling. She repeated several times that maybe Santa couldn't afford such a pricey item and would I possibly settle for . . .

I said nothing—just nodded my head. My stomach knotted up. Really? Santa had a budget? I knew we did. We weren't the poorest family in town, but I knew Dad worried about money because I overheard him telling Mom his concerns for a happy Christmas this year. Being a rancher, he only got paid once a year—in October after selling the calves. Often that money paid off loans he'd gotten to cover yearly expenses.

Santa had money concerns, too—oh, no! That caught me by surprise. I knew I was in trouble because Mom revisited this topic again and again in the next couple of weeks, trying to protect me from a deep disappointment. She realized how much I wanted that desk—more than any doll or toy I had ever asked for before.

"Don't be disappointed!" she repeated. How

could I not be! Until this point, you always came through each Christmas. I dreaded Christmas Eve last year because I knew that specific desk I'd dreamed of wouldn't be under/near the tree for me. And it wasn't.

Santa, you replaced it with a tacky metal desk with no drawers—only two shelves, one under the top of it and one near the bottom. It didn't even look like a desk—no wood, no drawers, no cubbies!

Mom watched my response with tears in her eyes. I hid my tears and broken heart last year, but I lost all faith in you, Santa. So, how do I write to you this year? Do I just make a general request? Can I be honest and say it doesn't matter because I don't believe anymore?

Help me out here on what to do. This is a pre-letter, so answer me please before I ask for something this year that I won't get!

Thank you,

Larada

I wrote this letter as an adult, but I remember the heartbreak of that Christmas and my wavering belief in Santa afterward.

Did Santa ever disappoint you at Christmas? If so, what did you do?

CHAPTER

TEN

GRANDMA'S HOMEMADE TURKEY & EGG NOODLES AND POPCORN BALLS

I have two favorite Christmas memories about my maternal grandmother—homemade turkey and egg noodles, and popcorn balls.

Every year, Grandma Dickerson, my mom's mother, made all the traditional sweets for Christmas time, but she made something not exactly "Christmasy" that became my favorite. Popcorn balls. She always prepared all those goodies before we arrived, so I never got to make them with her, and I never found out how she made them.

Still, the popcorn balls live on. I found a great recipe in the Folsom Garden Club cookbook from Folsom, New Mexico, and while it's not the same, I've used it every year since. (See recipe in Appendix A.) Every Christmas I make two batches of popcorn balls—a red and a green batch. I love making these sweet treats, and as I munch on them, Grandma Dickerson comes to mind. I don't have her recipe, but I have my memories.

The other memory I have is the day after Christmas, Grandma made homemade turkey and egg noodles. Being of the generation that didn't waste a thing, she boiled the turkey carcass from the day before to get a good broth for the soup.

Then she would make the homemade noodles. She never used a bowl; she poured out a mound of flour on the table, scooped out the center to make a crater, then started adding ingredients. Once the dough was mixed, she would roll out the noodles and cut them and leave them scattered on the table to dry for a while. They looked like a tangle of lost spirits!

Grandma was a short lady, so I stood at her elbow, often watching the process, anticipating the finished product. She knew it was my favorite dish, so she spoiled me with this treat any Christmas we were at her house.

I had enjoyed all the trimmings of the Christmas dinner, but the savory smell of the turkey broth cooking the next day signaled what lay ahead. The knowledge of the dish coming had my mouth watering. The sampling of the broth, the aroma of turkey cooking, and the steam of the hot soup warmed my heart and soul.

I have never tried to make her noodles—again I don't have her recipe. I'm not sure she had one. Maybe I should google a recipe for homemade noodles and try my hand at a batch. I'm sure all those years at her side would help me create something special.

Mom was always a part of this special time in the kitchen. Grandma was a skilled cook, and these two Christmas memories warm me every holiday time. It was a communal time in the kitchen—three generations enjoying each other around one tradition I miss today and one I've continued.

Do you have a favorite "Grandma Christmas memory"?

CHAPTER

ELEVEN

CUTTING DOWN OUR CHRISTMAS TREE

We never bought a Christmas tree when I was growing up. Why would we? Growing up in southeastern Colorado, we could choose a tree on our family ranch to become our star Christmas tree every year —free for the selection and lots of fun.

Mom and I would start looking for the year's Christmas tree in October, during hunting season, as we walked the canyons, measuring trees in our minds.

"There's the perfect one." Mom pointed to a small three-foot piñon pine tree that she wanted to put up on the coffee table. She went on and on about the virtues of a small tree. Dad, Bub, my brother, and I moaned and groaned. Oh, not this again, but we knew her—she always wanted a small tree, and we didn't.

Driving a little farther near the canyon, I spotted a regal six-foot piñon pine tree and exclaimed, "Here it is! Let's mark this one. This is it, for sure—our Christmas tree for this year."

Dad and Bub nodded their heads in agreement. We continued our lighthearted banter back and forth about small trees versus big trees. Then we would continue our task of hunting for a deer to have venison for the winter.

This routine repeated itself throughout the months of October and November and into the beginning of December if Dad or Bub didn't get a deer. With the three of us outnumbering her, Mom often lost the tree size debate.

One year, though, we three "big Christmas tree lovers" overdid ourselves.

It was early December, and the time had come to cut down our tree. For some reason, Mom didn't go—too busy baking our fudge, divinity, and other Christmas goodies. Without her there, the three of us could choose a big tree that year with no fuss. We scouted out the ones I had mentally marked throughout the fall, but Dad and Bub spied one they wanted that wasn't on the list. The saw came out, and they cut it down as a team, laughing about how Mom would react.

Yes, it looked fabulous out on the ranch against the deep blue sky and the snow drifts surrounding it. We admired our tree and laughed about Mom's possible response. What added to the joy of our selection—it was our first year in our new home with much higher ceilings, so the taller the tree, the better.

As we drove home, we prepared for Mom's comments, rehearsing our answers to her probing questions. We drove up to the front of our house and backed the pickup into the driveway so it would be easier to get the tree out. Already Dad and Bub had lamented about the sticky sap on their hands.

My part of the plan was to distract Mom while the guys brought the tree up. I hurried up the walk to get to Mom before she could see what we brought. She stuck her head out the door, quizzing me about the size. Kidding her, I replied, "It's your size." Her laugh told me she didn't believe it.

Normally Dad could carry our tree by himself, but it took both Dad and Bub to carry this one up the sidewalk and lay it on the front porch. As I stood measuring the tree in my mind, the tree seemed to go on forever.

Dad retrieved his hacksaw from the pickup and cut the bottom of the stump off evenly, a usual practice to fit it in the tree stand. The savory pine sap aroma filled the air. Still on its side, he easily slid it into the stand, tightened the bolts, and they stood it up. In our excitement to find the best tree, and thinking our ceiling higher than it was, we made a major mistake!

I held the screen door open, but already I realized we were in trouble. Bub and Dad wrestled to get the tree through the door. They tried to carry it upright in the stand, but it wouldn't fit, so they laid it out lengthwise and finally shoved it through. Thank God it was freshly cut or pine needles would have scattered everywhere!

Mom watched this show with amusement but was wise enough not to say anything. Dad and Bub set the stand on the floor by the front window, which Mom had cleared to showcase our tree to the passing traffic, and raised the tree.

All four of us gasped at the same time—the tree reached the ceiling and curled down at least a foot! What were we to do now?

Mom finally chimed in, "Don't forget to leave room for the star on top."

Dad took control. "That's easily fixed." He and Bub wrestled the tree out the door again. Once it was on the porch, Dad cut a foot and a half off the stump of the tree, and a few lower branches, and brought the shortened tree in and set it up. Dad's precision cut allowed just enough room for our traditional angel on top.

We stood back and admired our beautiful six-foot-plus piñon pine tree. Already its aromatic fragrance filled the room. Our decorations were stacked in boxes nearby, so now the fun of decorating began.

After our sigh of relief and chuckles, Mom took one last look at our tree before decorating and said, "Next year I'm for sure going with you three so we can get a smaller tree."

We all laughed, happy with our selection.

CHAPTER

TWELVE

A CHRISTMAS SAD AND PRECIOUS

It was in the late 1960s. Mom, Dad, my teenage brother, and I arrived in Poway, California for a special Christmas celebration. My sister's husband had recently been diagnosed with cirrhosis of the liver, and the future loomed bleak. This was only the second time we'd traversed to California for Christmas, and this trip had such a mixture of emotion.

A couple years before, as newlyweds, my sister, her new husband, and his two children came to Colorado for a truly country Christmas with lots of snow.

My new brother-in-law immediately started picking on me, and we bonded deeply even though he forced me to try cranberries—I had never tried this dish before. In reality, it wasn't a dish—Mom opened cranberry sauce that slid out of the can whole—plop!—and served it. It always looked slimy to me. With his humor and persistent influence, I grew to love cranberries!

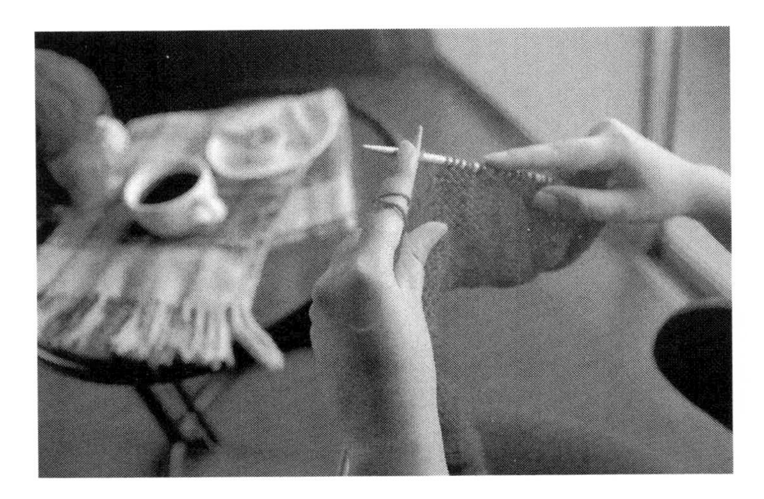

Sunny California appeared gloomy and heavy. The festive atmosphere of Christmas felt tinged with a deep sadness and fear. My sister greeted us warmly, knitting like a crazy woman. She shared with me that all of their gifts this year were knitted. I thought it a wonderful idea, but shortly I learned finances drove her decision.

I gasped silently at the man we saw on arrival, a shadow of the man we met a few short years ago. The disease had ravaged my brother-in-law's body, and he had lost so much weight, his clothes hung loose and limp on his frame.

But his spirit of love and laughter prevailed. Mom tried her hand at making homemade pie crusts, forgetting the effect of being at sea level on a recipe usually done at 6,100 feet above sea level. She grumbled about the gooey mess she kept trying to roll out, and my brother-in-law teased her unmercifully. As he ducked out of the kitchen with his latest quip, she slung the ball of dough at him, hitting him in the eye—a magnificent bullseye. Our laughter filled the kitchen with delight in the ridiculous.

Christmas Eve morning came, and my brother-in-law

slipped into Mom and Dad's bedroom and whispered his plan for the day to Mom and me. "I'm going to go sell some wood so I can buy my loving wife some Christmas presents. Don't let her know where I've gone. Can you help me wrap the presents when I get home?"

Mom and I both choked back tears, nodding our heads.

The impact of my brother-in-law's health had destroyed their finances. He hadn't worked his normal construction job in several months; my sister had a good job, but she was so busy and overwhelmed being a caregiver, too. Living in the wooded area of Poway, he cut wood whenever he could and sold it to make some extra money and to keep active—his current lack of working was not his nature.

Christmas Eve day went by uneventfully except for my sister's repeated refrain, "Where is my husband? What is he doing?" Her distress weighed on me, but I couldn't ruin his surprise. She continued to knit, the needles rapidly moving in her nervous hands.

Daylight slowly faded into darkness. Mom and I

exchanged worried glances all day—Dad and Bub joined my sister in wondering about the whereabouts of my brother-in-law.

Mom and I went to their bedroom to talk about what we should do—the pending darkness scared us. He had been gone for hours. What if something went wrong? Quietly my brother-in-law opened the door of my parent's bedroom, a couple bags in hand. He looked exhausted but pleased with himself.

We wrapped the small collection of gifts—all kitchen utensils for my sister. We placed the gifts under the tree, and my sister, contrite in her reaction to her husband's day-long absence, held back tears and pain.

I knew deep in my heart that this was the most precious exhibition of love I'd ever seen. His generosity and spirit graced the rest of that holiday.

Sixty-some years ago, and it still brings a smile to my heart, yet a tear to my eyes, as I remember his mission of love and the true spirit of Christmas.

Have you had a Christmas like this—both sweet and bittersweet at the same time?

CHAPTER THIRTEEN

ARE HOLIDAY TRADITIONS IMPORTANT?

I'm a tradition-based person—I love the familiar and the repetitious. As a child, our homespun traditions centered on our family. We cut down our own Christmas tree on our family ranch. We used to have lots of snow, so it was cold and messy but joyful and an adventure. I often had sticky sap all over my hands.

Because we didn't have a lot of money, presents were few and heartfelt. I wrote letters to Santa and dreamed about my gifts, looked at a Sears & Roebuck or Monkey Ward catalog and dog-eared pages so I could revisit them often.

I dressed up in my homemade Christmas outfit that Mom

had labored over for hours, and we ate Christmas Eve dinner at my grandparents' house across town. When we got to the car to leave for dinner, often Dad forgot something and went back inside to retrieve it. Later I realized that's when Santa came!

When we arrived, my grandparents' house filled quickly with our family and my aunt and uncle's family. Often our two great aunts from Tulsa, Oklahoma joined us and gave us $2 bills because one of them worked at a bank. The highlight of the evening was Granddad leading a parade of children from the front door to the back after he shouted, "I saw Santa Claus!"

We would return to our home after eating a savory dinner and opening our presents to see that Santa had visited us, and I realized my dreams. We opened our gifts and late into the evening played with our toys. Our tradition!

Christmas Day was low-key and filled with hours of playing with my new toys.

This scenario repeated itself most years, developing into the deep family traditions I love.

As an adult, the magic of Santa changed, but Christmas continued to be a wonderful time for me as I created new grown-up traditions. From my ex-husband, I added Midnight Mass on Christmas Eve at an Episcopal church to my Christmas traditions, and once again, church became a regular part of my celebration.

After my ex-husband and I divorced, Dad and Mom joined me in this tradition, and we drove to the Lutheran church in Trinidad, Colorado each Christmas Eve for Midnight Mass. Some of our most memorable conversations happened on those late-night fifty-mile drives home, sipping coffee and swapping stories.

As a middle school teacher for twenty-seven years, I put together a varied collection of holiday T-shirts, sweatshirts, pants, and jewelry that I started wearing the Monday after Thanksgiving—I'm still adding to this collection today. This was a time teachers could don Christmas-wear, and everyone enjoyed it. Walking down the hall with my bell necklace jingling, my students said I couldn't surprise them. They knew I was coming!

I love writing our Christmas letter, which features what we've done for the year. This last is my 35th year of writing it, and I enjoy the process of looking back and summarizing the year's activities and sharing lots of pictures from the year.

I cherish baking Christmas candy and goodies because it reminds me of Mom and all the fun we had in the kitchen—I use a lot of her delicious recipes. And I love sending Christmas cards. I don't receive that many anymore, but as I address each card, I'm flooded with memories of each person on my list, and it's a celebration of my family and friends.

The last tradition I will share is one my mom started in 1988. I was going to codependency treatment on December 22, 1988, and I wouldn't be home for Christmas. What a sad, stark time that was! She put together ten Advent gifts—one to open each day before Christmas, starting on December 15th. I packed the remaining gifts to take with me to treatment but when I entered the treatment facility, I had the shock of my life. I thought I would continue the daily tradition. They went through my bags, opened each of the wrapped gifts and thought a bag of potpourri was marijuana. Later, they did, however, give me the opened "safe" gifts. Even though I lost the opportunity to open those remaining Advent gifts, I felt Mom's presence in a special way that Christmas with those gifts.

We continued that tradition until she died, and I joined in the gift exchange and gave her little nonsensical gifts. Later, we added Aunt Willie and Lin—they enjoyed this tradition, too.

The various traditions have blessed me deeply and shaped me into the person I am during the holidays. Merry Christmas to you and yours!

Are similar traditions like mine important to you? Do you have any different ones?

SCRIPTURE – LUKE 2:10

Luke 2:10 *And the angel said to them,*
"Fear not, for behold, I bring you good news
of great joy that will be for all the people.

CHAPTER FOURTEEN

CHRISTMAS CAROLING IN MY TWENTIES

I continued the Christmas caroling activity from my youth into my twenties. My ex-husband (let's call him Rudolph) and I moved to Loveland, Colorado in the late 70s and attended All Saints Episcopal Church. At that time, several couples our age attended our church, and we did lots of activities together. And our whole church was very active.

When Christmas came around our first year there, someone suggested Christmas caroling. Immediately I returned to my caroling experience in Branson, Colorado, and I whole-heartedly agreed, "Let's do it!"

Someone from the congregation provided a flatbed trailer, and we stacked bales of hay on it to sit on. The much-anticipated night arrived, and I layered and bundled up! Yes, this would be fantastic.

I loved the multi-generational participation of our church. We had older people, teenagers, and young couples with their children. We had all ages!

I knew it was cold, but singing familiar Christmas songs and the fellowship warmed me through and through—until we stopped in front of a bank and saw the temperature on its marquee: six degrees below zero! I heard a collective gasp as we realized how cold it was! At the sight of that thermometer, the songs and fellowship no longer warmed us.

See, Loveland is about 250 miles north of Branson, where I grew up, and that makes a lot of difference in the weather. In Loveland, we got lots more snow and colder weather. When I thought of Christmas caroling, I thought of the cold of southeastern Colorado, not northern Colorado.

Immediately, my face froze. My fingers and toes tingled, and I gasped—six degrees below zero! Numb and painful!

Others near me stomped their feet and seemed to react to the low temperature. We still had several stops before hot chocolate and cookies.

Pulling my snow cap down over my ears, I snuggled close to the people sitting next to me. Then I wrapped my scarf around my head and mouth. Turning to my friend next to me, I only saw eyes peeping through her cap and scarf; we laughed at our get-ups. I pulled the wool blanket draped over my legs up to my chin.

I continued singing my familiar Christmas songs as best I could, even though I started to shiver with the cold. I noticed our singing had become muffled. I looked around, and everyone with a scarf had it wrapped around their mouths. Children had moved in close to their parents, seeking warmth and comfort. Somehow, those familiar songs didn't warm me the way they did before I knew how cold it was outside!

I suffered through the rest of the evening, but the extreme cold made the reward of the hot chocolate and cookies at the end that much more warming and delicious. After warming up when the crowd dispersed, a festive air remained. But I still shudder at that thermometer reading and the hours I sat on that trailer, cold to the bone! Yet I was happy out Christmas caroling!

That was the last time I did Christmas caroling outside in the cold, sitting on a bale of hay. I have moved to a warmer part of the world—New Mexico—but caroling never came up here. I cherish that memory from so long ago, but not the cold!

CHAPTER FIFTEEN

PARENTS' SHOPPING NIGHT OUT!

In 1979, as a mid-twenties couple in Loveland, Colorado, my ex-husband, Rudolph and I hung out with couples from our church, All Saints Episcopal Church. Some couples our same age had started their families, and we'd babysat some of their kids in our home. We both took the time to play with the children at church, with them often running to hug us during the Coffee Hour afterward. We watched the mounting stress for their parents as the holidays approached, yet we yearned for our own child.

As Thanksgiving approached, wives talked to me about juggling working and Christmas shopping without their children in tow. Already overwhelmed with the prospects of the holiday ahead, they also lamented about no time alone with their husbands during this busy time of year. I reflected on the ample time I had to prepare for the holiday.

Then I had an idea: how about we take the children of the four couples we regularly hung out with for one evening from 5:00–10:00 p.m. No strings attached. All the couples had to do was drop off their children, have a dinner out, and shop. Rudolph immediately agreed.

To begin with, I sent off the invitations for "A Parents' Night Out" with a request to call with their RSVP. This was prior to email and text messaging. We had a hundred percent participation: we would have five children ranging from four to seven years old, and they all knew us so no problem with a reluctant participant. That gave me some idea of how to plan the evening.

So, the prep work began. We bought a piñata filled with candy and attached it to a spare broomstick. I bought hot dogs to roast. Also, I bought marshmallows, Hershey bars, and graham crackers for S'mores. I purchased construction paper and glitter to make cards for the kids to create for their parents. Then my current favorite Christian Christmas song, "Come on Ring Those Belles" by Evie prompted me to buy jingle bells, and I put three to four bells together and created a jingle bell strip. A great plan was unfolding!

As our event drew near, I felt the mounting anticipation both from the children and their parents. Each time I saw them at church, the parents quizzed us about what we had planned, would it be too much, etc. And the children jumped in our laps, excited and ready for a fun-filled evening. I knew it would be a great evening for us, the children, and their parents.

When the parents arrived with their children, we greeted each couple, then quickly sent them on their way. We had lots to do! In the process, I had shared my plan with another couple from the church, Jim and Merrilou, who had no children at the time, and they quickly volunteered to help, and boy, did we need them before the night was over.

We began the evening with roasting the hot dogs in our fireplace. In the background, we had Christmas music playing. Rudolph had crafted long sticks for each child to roast his/her own. We used paper plates and had the children sit on the floor in front of the fireplace to enjoy the crackling fire. For dessert, we roasted marshmallows, then stuck them between graham crackers with a chunk of Hershey's chocolate. That was a gooey mess, but the children loved them.

One young girl exclaimed, "I've never made S'mores before!"

After cleaning off sticky fingers, we jumped into the next activity. Because the weather was mild this Christmas, we moved the group out to the patio. As Rudolph held up the piñata, Jim and Merrilou blindfolded each participant. I gave them a bat to try to hit the piñata, but they repeatedly hit

Rudolph's hands instead, by working their way up the broomstick to where he was holding it. Finally, I helped one blindfolded child crash it open, and candy went flying. We gave each a zip lock bag to put their candy in, and they each fared well. Afterward, my ex-husband questioned this activity, shaking his hands, but he still had a smile on his face.

Next, each child created a Christmas card for their parents using the glitter and construction paper I had bought. Many didn't know how to write yet, so the four adults helped them write a message on the front and then helped with the signature inside. Next, we gave them glitter and glue to decorate the card—what a mess! We had turned our wooden dining room chairs around to use as tables for the children, and the glitter haphazardly ended up on the seats of the chairs. In fact, when I sold those chairs years later, I still saw traces of glitter here and there—a souvenir of an amazing evening.

To calm the night down after all the activities, we ended the evening with the lights down low and only our Christmas tree lights on. We sang Christmas carols trying to bring down the energy, but Evie's "Come on Ring Those Bells"[1] and my jingle bell strips revved them up again. They danced around shaking the bells, singing "Come on ring those bells" over and over again. What had I started?

When the parents joined us, we drank homemade wassail and finished the night with a couple calmer carols. The children looked exhausted; my fellow workers felt exhausted. And the parents looked refreshed—exactly the result I wanted!

---

1. https://www.youtube.com/watch?v=Ygzvcy2B9jw

CHAPTER SIXTEEN

WHAT'S YOUR FAVORITE CHRISTMAS MEMORY?

Favorite Christmas memory—I have so many, but one stands out that has affected my whole life.

When I was four or five years old, my mom made me a beautiful white dress with red embroidery on the top for Christmas. I remember her laboring over it because sewing didn't come naturally to her. I tried it on, and the gathered waistline with the fitted bodice just didn't please her. It didn't lie the way it should, so she ripped it out several times. She didn't have one of those fancy sewing machines they have today that gathers easily—she gathered it all by hand. She so wanted to complete it for our Christmas Eve family get-together, so her efforts continued, and I continued to try it on, hoping this time it worked.

I felt so special about her choosing to sew this for me. With mounting anticipation, I obsessed about wearing it on Christmas Eve. As usual, the Horner family celebration happened at my grandparents', with a multitude of relatives in attendance.

For weeks, Mom sewed my lovely white dress, then ripped out her mistakes and cried. I had such mixed emotions over this project. I wanted it finished on time, but I didn't want my mom so stressed out.

After all her hard work, Mom finished my special dress. I donned my miracle dress and saw the relief in her eyes! She took me to the mirror. I saw Cinderella in my reflection! I loved it!

When Dad got home from the ranch, I had to model it for him, and he oohed and aahed over it, solidifying the fact the lovely dress had transformed me into a magical princess!

~

As a square dancer, the moment I don my gorgeous square dance outfit, I'm transported back to that moment as a child when I put on my beautiful Christmas dress Mom made. I am Cinderella, ready for the ball.

If you look at the square dance attire for women and think how baffling, let me tell you. Once I put on my outfit and petticoat and pettipants and twirl in front of the mirror, I am transformed. My feminine side comes out, and I love it!

I don't remember any gifts from the year Mom made that dress, but I remember her efforts and tenacity. I recall that precious dress and the feeling I had when I walked in the door at my grandparents' house and the reception I received! That's a gift you can't wrap! This is my favorite Christmas memory of all time!

Because of the power of this memory, as an adult, I have made many Christmas presents. Whether I knitted a stocking or a sweater, painted a plastercraft cowboy statue, or crafted a family calendar. The joy for me is the making and the giving. I learned this from my mother's wonderful dress project.

During the pandemic, I knitted twenty-plus dish clothes and gave them as gifts to my family. I value this life-saving therapy. While I knitted a simple rhythmic pattern that soothed my soul in the movement, I relaxed and let go of the time we experienced. Those dish clothes blessed me and hopefully will bless the recipient.

So, a delightful Christmas memory touched me deeply as a child and continues every time I dance and every Christmas gift I create. You can't beat that!

Do you have a favorite Christmas memory that has affected your whole life? How old were you? How did it affect you?

CHAPTER

SEVENTEEN

HOMEMADE CHRISTMAS—I LOVE IT!

Homemade Christmas decorations and gifts have always given me a lot of pleasure in the making! From knitting stockings to painting plastercraft figurines to computer generating annual family calendars (see in Chapter 25 *Christmas Shopping During the Pandemic?*), I have made quite a variety and enjoyed the hours making everything.

KNITTED CHRISTMAS STOCKINGS

I started knitting in 4-H when I was ten years old and still enjoy this productive hobby today. Many years ago, I found a fantastic Christmas stocking pattern and made my first. Then I branched out, making my nieces and nephew their own with their names on them.

The tradition continues. First, I knitted a stocking each for my nephew and nieces, then their children, and now *their* children—three generations!

I didn't limit my production of Christmas stockings to just family. Because of our close relationship, I made my best friend's children each one, and over the years, I have knitted so many for other friends, I lost count!

One Christmas many years ago, my best friend posted her family picture on Facebook, and there in the background hung the Christmas stockings I'd made, and how festive they looked! My reaction: goose bumps!

To make these colorful holiday stockings, I always use red, white, and green yarn or variegated yarn, but I don't plan out the color scheme until I start. I have to graph out the name on graph paper so it will fit on half of the stocking, so that takes some designing for sure. You can see my name almost doesn't fit. I learned from mine a trick to make long names fit!

What a truly wonderful experience it is to finish a stocking. Then I add my professional-looking label on the inside that says, "From the knitting needles of Larada Horner-Miller."

PAINTED PLASTERCRAFT FIGURINES

Mr. & Mrs. Santa Claus

As a young married couple in 1973, my ex-husband and I didn't have any Christmas decorations and not much money to buy them. My mom loved to do crafts, and I inherited her interest in working with my hands. I had seen such beautiful ceramic Christmas decorations, but again the money issues of newlyweds, so I found out about plastercraft. ". . . similar to ceramics, but there is no firing or kiln necessary. Simply use easy water-based acrylic paints."[1]

The first year I made Santa and loved the whimsical look he has on his face with his wink. The next year I added Mrs. Claus, busy knitting. My kind of woman!

I had to be careful in painting a large figurine like this. Being mindful of the size, I had to be systematic about the colors and letting them dry. And I had to be careful not to drop them! The final spray I used to set the color always intrigued me because it added such a dazzling finish to my project. It looked like a ceramic piece!

Over the years, I've protected my favorite Christmas plastercraft figurines in my many moves. After Christmas, I always placed them on a shelf in a spare bedroom to make sure they didn't befall any issues being stored. When I married Lin, he wanted to store them in trunks in a shed, and I panicked. Luckily, he wraps them up carefully, and they have fared well these last eleven years.

My Christmas Tree

After my success with Santa and Mrs. Claus, the next year I moved on to a lighted Christmas tree. The original tree was small, so I bought an extension to make it bigger! Every year, I love putting the little light bulbs in the spots and marvel at how pretty it is lit up.

I keep the small colored bulbs in a zip lock bag and enjoy putting them on the tree, making sure I spread out all the colors evenly. This is another item I have kept stored safely, so it looks pristine!

Since Lin and I married, we put this tree up in our bedroom, and it's a pleasant light to go to bed and see!

Almost fifty years later, I continue to enjoy these three items as they remind me of our many years together.

. . .

Latch Hook Kit I Made

Here's another craft of mine! I thoroughly enjoyed latch hook for many years. I bought the kits, finished the pattern, and created ways to hang them. For Christmas, I did this Noel hanging and also a Christmas wreath. These two decorations adorned my living room and hallway.

WOODEN CHRISTMAS ORNAMENTS

My story about my wooden Christmas ornaments appears in Chapter 25, *Bobby Pins & Christmas Ornaments.*

I LOVE MAKING homemade Christmas decorations and gifts. As I set out the decorations I've made, I get nostalgic remembering sitting at the table so long ago and making them. With each stitch I knit or photo I place, I have the joy of thinking about the gift and the person I made it for.

How about you? Do you make anything for Christmas gifts? If so, what?

---

1. [1https://www.plastercraft.com/#:~:text=Plastercrafts%20are%20similar%20to%20ceramics,easy%20water%20based%20acrylic%20paints

CHAPTER
EIGHTEEN
GIVE AWAY A CHRISTMAS TREE?

Giveaway a Christmas tree? Why would anyone do that? When I first came to Albuquerque, New Mexico in 1991 as a middle school teacher, I started a tradition in my classroom. Each year, I put up a Christmas tree, then gave it away to one of my students before our Christmas vacation.

Early in December, I'd have my students put their names in a hat, and we'd draw the lucky winner. I taught in a low-income school and many of my students' families struggled with the basics. A Christmas tree was a luxury and a fresh-cut one, a novelty.

In 1991, and throughout the time I taught, we could still put up a Christmas tree in our classrooms, and I dressed in my Christmas outfits, starting the first Monday after Advent. Today, I know that teachers can't do this, which makes me sad. That Christmas tree always brought a touch of magic into my classroom—the piñon pine smell, the twinkling lights, and the popcorn chain we threaded together in each class and laughed over.

Often, I would turn down the overhead lights and read to my classes with just the Christmas tree lights on. What a precious memory!

Because I put the tree up at the beginning of December, the anticipation grew about the contest. I teased them often with the possibility: who would win? All students were eligible!

I will never forget that first year of seeing the lucky student whose name I drew. He was the winner! Shocked, he and several students helped me un-decorate the tree after our class Christmas party. Then he convinced two friends to help him carry the tree home. As I looked out the window and watched this funny parade, the smiles and excitement the group exhibited warmed my heart. Even though they were middle-schoolers, they treasured this fresh-cut tree. After that first year, I knew I had found a grand tradition to continue!

. . .

HOW DID I come about having an extra tree each year to give away?

After I moved to Albuquerque, I often went home to Colorado for Thanksgiving. Like I mentioned before, my parents had a family ranch in southeastern Colorado and northeastern New Mexico. Growing up, we went out to the ranch and cut our own tree each year.

During that weekend home, we went out to the ranch and cut down three trees—one for my folks, one for my home, and one for my classroom. My parents loved the idea of providing a Christmas tree for my classroom and they loved the gifting to a student.

I loved those trips out to our ranch, cutting down a fresh tree. Dad, Mom, and I made a great excursion out of it. On previous trips out there, we had already decided where the best piñon pine trees were. During these years, Dad started the sawing, but because of his breathing issues and his age, I usually helped. And yes, we always got sap on our hands—what a delicious smell, but a sticky mess!

I felt privileged to give away a Christmas tree to one of my students, and this tradition continued for many years. What a rewarding experience it was!

Is a Christmas tree giveaway something special? I thought it was, especially after seeing my students' smiles. Have you ever given a Christmas tree away? If so, what was the effect?

CHAPTER

NINETEEN

WHY CELEBRATE THE TWELVE DAYS OF CHRISTMAS?

We hear this song, "The Twelve Days of Christmas," every holiday season many times. To many, it's a mystery what it means.

"The Twelve Days of Christmas" has strong liturgical ties to the Catholic and the Anglican church, which is my church, the Episcopal church. I cherish the celebratory nature of stretching the Christmas season out for twelve days instead of one day only. I mean, we work so hard preparing for it, it should be more than twenty-four hours!

"The 12 days of Christmas is the period that in Christian theology marks the span between the birth of Christ and the coming of the Magi, the three Wise Men. It begins on December 25 (Christmas) and runs through January 6 (the Epiphany, sometimes also called Three Kings' Day)."[1]

Another explanation for this song is based in the Catholic church: "'The Twelve Days of Christmas' was written in England as one of the 'catechism songs' to help young Catholics learn the tenets of their faith—a memory aid, when to be caught with anything in *writing* indicating adherence to the Catholic faith could not only get you imprisoned, it could get you hanged, or shortened by a head—or hanged, drawn, and quartered, a rather peculiar and ghastly punishment I'm not aware was ever practiced anywhere else."[2]

I love this song and the idea that Christmas lasts for twelve days. So when the rest of the world takes down their decorations and folds away their favorite Christmas leggings the day after Christmas, I don't. I continue enjoying my decorations, twinkling lights, and wearing my colorful Christmas outfits for twelve full days!

HERE ARE the traditional words of this favorite song:

The 12 Days of Christmas

On the first day of Christmas,

My true love gave to me:
A partridge in a pear tree.

On the second day of Christmas,

My true love gave to me:
Two turtle doves,
and a partridge in a pear tree.

~

On the third day of Christmas,

My true love gave to me:
Three French hens,
Two turtle doves,
and a partridge in a pear tree.

~

On the fourth day of Christmas,

My true love gave to me:
Four calling birds,
Three French hens,
Two turtle doves,
and a partridge in a pear tree.

On the fifth day of Christmas,

My true love gave to me:
Five golden rings!
Four calling birds,
Three French hens,
Two turtle doves,
and a partridge in a pear tree.

. . .

On the sixth day of Christmas,

My true love gave to me:
Six geese a-laying,
Five golden rings!
Four calling birds,
Three French hens,
Two turtle doves,
and a partridge in a pear tree.

On the seventh day of Christmas,

My true love gave to me:

Seven swans a-swimming,
Six geese a-laying,
Five golden rings!
Four calling birds,
Three French hens,
Two turtle doves,
and a partridge in a pear tree.

On the eighth day of Christmas,

My true love gave to me:
Eight maids a-milking,
Seven swans a-swimming,
Six geese a-laying,
Five golden rings!
Four calling birds,
Three French hens,
Two turtle doves,
and a partridge in a pear tree.

On the ninth day of Christmas,

My true love gave to me:
Nine ladies dancing,
Eight maids a-milking,
Seven swans a-swimming,
Six geese a-laying,
Five golden rings!
Four calling birds,
Three French hens,
Two turtle doves,
and a partridge in a pear tree.

On the tenth day of Christmas,

My true love gave to me:
Ten lords a-leaping,
Nine ladies dancing,
Eight maids a-milking,
Seven swans a-swimming,
Six geese a-laying,
Five golden rings!
Four calling birds,
Three French hens,
Two turtle doves,
and a partridge in a pear tree.

On the eleventh day of Christmas,

My true love gave to me:
Eleven pipers piping,
Ten lords a-leaping,
Nine ladies dancing,
Eight maids a-milking,
Seven swans a-swimming,
Six geese a-laying,
Five golden rings!
Four calling birds,

Three French hens,
Two turtle doves,
and a partridge in a pear tree.

On the twelfth day of Christmas,

My true love gave to me:
Twelve drummers drumming,
Eleven pipers piping,
Ten lords a-leaping,
Nine ladies dancing,
Eight maids a-milking,
Seven swans a-swimming,
Six geese a-laying,
Five golden rings!
Four calling birds,
Three French hens,
Two turtle doves,
and a partridge in a pear tree.[3]

GRAB A STEAMING cup of coffee or tea, relax in your favorite chair near your Christmas tree, and listen to the traditional song for a moment: https://www.youtube.com/watch?v=2Fe11OlMiz8

It leaves me feeling light and happy! The delightful repetition grabs my heart.

~

I LIVE IN NEW MEXICO, so here's a regional humorous take on this familiar song:

12 Days of Christmas (New Mexico Style)

On the first day of Christmas, my true love gave to me . . .

A roadrunner in a piñon tree

~

On the second day of Christmas, my true love gave to me . . .

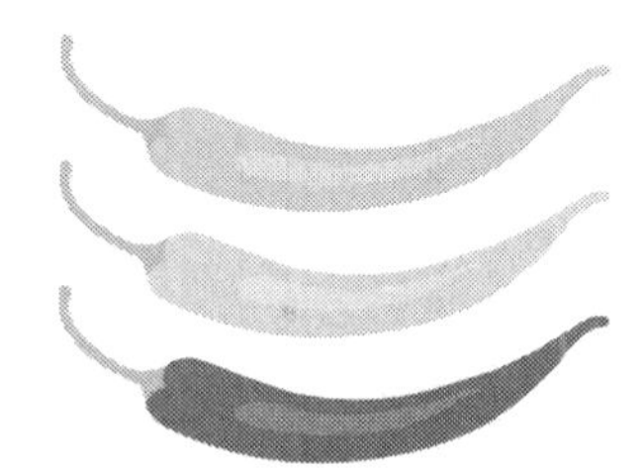

Red and green chiles
    And a roadrunner in a piñon tree.

On the third day of Christmas, my true love gave to me . . .

Three lift tickets
    Red and green chiles
    And a roadrunner in a piñon tree

On the fourth day of Christmas, my true love gave to me . . .

Four hot air balloons
Three lift tickets
Red and green chiles
And a roadrunner in a piñon tree

On the fifth day of Christmas, my true love gave to me . . .

Five turquoise rings!
Four hot air balloons
Three lift tickets
Red and green chiles
And a roadrunner in a piñon tree

On the sixth day of Christmas, my true love gave to me . . .

Six sopaipillas
  Five turquoise rings!
  Four hot air balloons
  Three lift tickets
  Red and green chiles
  And a roadrunner in a piñon tree

On the seventh day of Christmas, my true love gave to me . . .

Seven bowls posole
  Six sopaipillas

Five turquoise rings!
Four hot air balloons
Three lift tickets
Red and green chiles
And a roadrunner in a piñon tree

On the eighth day of Christmas, my true love gave to me . . .

Eight bright red ristras
Seven bowls posole
Six sopaipillas
Five turquoise rings!
Four hot air balloons
Three lift tickets
Red and green chiles
And a roadrunner in a piñon tree

On the ninth day of Christmas, my true love gave to me . . .

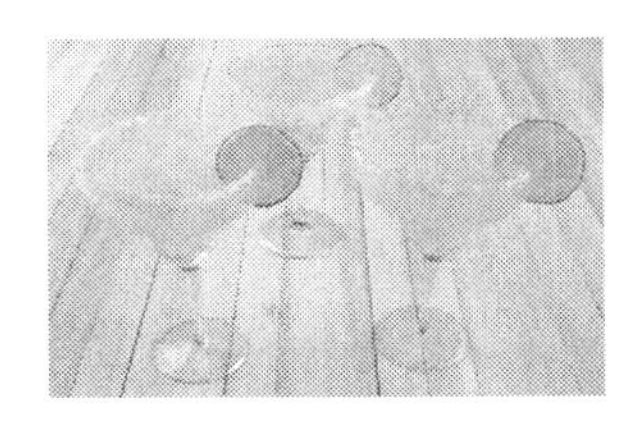

Nine margaritas
Eight bright red ristras
Seven bowls posole
Six sopaipillas
Five turquoise rings!
Four hot air balloons
Three lift tickets
Red and green chiles
And a roadrunner in a piñon tree

On the tenth day of Christmas, my true love gave to me . . .

Ten pork tamales
Nine margaritas
Eight bright red ristras
Seven bowls posole
Six sopaipillas
Five turquoise rings!
Four hot air balloons
Three lift tickets

Red and green chiles
And a roadrunner in a piñon tree

On the eleventh day of Christmas, my true love gave to me . . .

Eleven biscochitos
Ten pork tamales
Nine margaritas
Eight bright red ristras
Seven bowls posole
Six sopaipillas
Five turquoise rings!
Four hot air balloons
Three lift tickets
Red and green chiles
And a roadrunner in a piñon tree

On the twelfth day of Christmas, my true love gave to me . . .

Twelve farolitos
Eleven bisochitos
Ten pork tamales
Nine margaritas
Eight bright red ristras
Seven bowls posole
Six sopaipillas
Five turquoise rings!
Four hot air balloons
Three lift tickets
Red and green chiles
And a roadrunner in a piñon tree . . .[4]

TAKE this information to heart and keep celebrating Christmas until January 6 this year, and you will enjoy a different spirit of Christmas. Then next year when you first hear this Christmas carol, remember this information and plan to celebrate the full twelve days.

---

1. https://www.vox.com/2015/12/25/10661878/12-days-of-christmas-explained
2. https://www.catholic.org/advent/advent.php?id=2
3. http://www.chiff.com/home_life/holiday/christmas/12-days-lyrics.htm
4. https://www.newmexico.org/nmmagazine/articles/post/12dayschristmas-79060/

SCRIPTURE – LUKE 2:12

Luke 2:12 *And this will be a sign for you: you will find a baby wrapped in swaddling cloths and lying in a manger.*

CHAPTER TWENTY

BOBBY PINS & CHRISTMAS ORNAMENTS

One of the things that takes me back to my childhood, no matter how old I get, is my Christmas decor. Throughout the years, I've enjoyed collecting my decorations, and just seeing each one brings a smile to my face. Some are traditional; many are not! Some are handmade; some are special gifts from friends and customers from my time as a beautician. When I put them out at Christmas time, I immediately connect with the person who gave them to me, or the time I sat and created them. The magic of Christmas memories!

MY GRANDMA'S GLASS ORNAMENTS WITH HER BOBBY PINS

When Grandma Horner died, Dad set out boxes of her things in the basement of her house. After all the other grandchildren went through her belongings, he threatened to throw the rest away. As her namesake, he had already given me a beautiful black onyx ring and bracelet she wore daily. I had thought that enough. But before he pitched the rest of her stuff, I took one last look. When I saw Grandma's Christmas decorations, I choked up, remembering all those Christmases and her ornaments on the trees. I chose her Christmas ornaments—three boxes of vintage ornaments I had seen yearly on her Christmas tree.

When I took them out to hang them the first year, I noticed something I'd never seen before. My Grandma Horner was ahead of her time! She used bobby pins to hang up her glass ornaments, decades before someone invented those great little ornament hangers we all know! And I've kept those precious bobby pins attached to many of her ornaments ever since! Her hand touched them as mine do when I hang them; no matter that she's gone—she is still here in her ornaments!

I'm sad to say several ornaments broke one year when my Christmas tree toppled over! But I still have about fifteen I hang every year, and every time I see them with their little bobby pins, I remember all our Christmases together, and my heart smiles.

MY SANTA DOLLAR BILL

In 1973 I passed my State Board tests to become a beautician —after a year-long program at Trinidad State Junior College. I worked for five years in Denver, Colorado, then I continued my profession when we moved to Loveland, Colorado in 1978

for nine more years. The last four of those years, I worked while attending Colorado State University to get my teaching degree.

As a beautician, I received tips as a part of my pay, and gladly did so! I had regular customers who came in every week and were like family to me.

In Loveland, Colorado in 1979, I received a surprising tip from one of my clients, Tex White: a dollar bill with a Santa Claus glued on the face of it—it looked real! Yes, Tex was an older woman from Texas, and I enjoyed her soft southern drawl every week. All four of the beauticians in the beauty salon looked forward to her humor and her entertaining stories.

I giggled as I placed it on my tree this year—forty years later—remembering the joke that Tex had pulled on me with this dollar bill! I had never seen anything like that! Every year, it's one of my favorite ornaments to decorate with.

A SAMPLING OF MY WOODEN ORNAMENTS

My ex-husband and I married in September 1973. When Christmas rolled around that year, we had little money and no decorations for our first tree.

So, I found an inexpensive kit of wooden ornaments that I painted, front and back. Each evening after work, I spread fresh newspaper on the card table I sent up in front of the TV and painted Mr. and Mrs. Santa Claus, Frosty the Snowman, an angel, Soldier, dove, and many other Christmas figures.

Switching from the black container to the green to the red, I ran back and forth to the sink to wash out the brush. Colorful paint spotted my hands, and I gathered up the newspapers every night when I finished and set the painted pieces out to dry.

Then I learned a system: I painted all the black on one and then on all of the rest. When I finished for the night, I laid them on the table to dry, knowing I'd pick up the next night with a different color. The system worked better, and I didn't run myself crazy.

Each year since then, I've enjoyed adding those simple ornaments to my tree, remembering how I felt when I finished the numerous decorations.

Now, I place these ornaments on the bottom branches because my cat, Jesse, loves to hide under the tree. If he knocks one off, it's safe and won't break! Inexpensive, yet priceless!

I have never wanted a perfectly trimmed Christmas tree; I prefer one loaded with ornaments and memories!

Recently, I have added ornaments from different trips and adventures. They also add to the eclectic feeling of my tree.

CHAPTER TWENTY-ONE

A SPECIAL GIFT

During my lifetime, I often helped Dad shop for Mom's Christmas gift, but in the mid-1980s, a tradition was born.

That special year, Dad asked me to pick out matching dresses for Mom and me for her and my Christmas gift. This started a tradition that continued even after he died, until Mom's death.

Any time we wore our matching outfits for Dad, his chest swelled. He smiled a lot and made a point of letting everyone around him know the history of this tradition. He was so proud!

Dad died on January 7, 1996. As that year inched closer to the holidays, Mom whispered to me in her grief one night, "You don't have to buy our look-alike outfits for Christmas anymore, do you?" We both sobbed. I shook my head, "YES," and I never wavered. I continued this heartfelt tradition.

Mom and I in our first Christmas Dress from Dad

Our first outfit was a dress, and during the years Dad was alive, I continued buying us dresses. After he died, I bought us a variety of outfits: slacks and sweaters, warm-up suits, and skirt and top outfits.

One problem I faced when I bought slacks—my mom's height. She was short; I'm short, too, but she was much shorter. I often had to look for our outfits in two different departments—women's and petite—and it was always a hard search! There were several times I would buy petite for both of us and just deal with shorter slacks than I preferred! After wearing those pairs for several years, all my pants shrunk to a length I felt embarrassed to wear, but I did anyway—it was our special outfit!

We wore our outfits together proudly and often explained why we were dressed alike. We always gave Dad the credit for starting this tradition.

When Mom passed away, getting rid of our look-alike outfits broke my heart! I couldn't imagine seeing them on someone else. Then I had an idea! I shipped them off to a girl-friend in Virginia who was Mom's height. I wouldn't have to see them again, but I still knew they'd be going to a good home. Those outfits were the first of Mom's clothes to go!

I did continue wearing mine, celebrating the connection to Mom and Dad. This tradition blessed my heart for many years.

Do you have anything like it in your family? Do you mind wearing an outfit that someone else has?

CHAPTER TWENTY-TWO

MY LOVE FOR CHRISTMAS EVE HAS REMAINED STRONG

I have always loved this night. My love for Christmas Eve goes way back to those big gatherings at my grandparents' house, the focus on Santa Claus and childhood joy. As the years unfolded, I've moved to and visited different cities during the holidays, so my celebration of Christmas Eve took on multiple denominational tones and the focus became the Christ child.

SAN DIEGO, CA

In 1972, my ex-husband, Rudolph joined us as we traveled to California to spend Christmas with my sisters and brother who lived there. It was his first time away from home at Christmas, so he needed the comfort of familiarity.

He suggested we go to Midnight Mass on Christmas Eve. My family didn't attend church, so it was just him and me, and this was my first Episcopal Christmas Eve. We found an Episcopal church close by and away we went, borrowing Dad's car.

When we arrived, poinsettia trees surrounded the church —I had never seen one before! I love poinsettias and buy one each year, but to see a tree fascinated me. Then the shock came. The church was under total renovation, and the windows were gone! Living in snowy Colorado, that seemed outrageous to us. As we sat and enjoyed the familiar service and songs, it felt good to be celebrating Christ's birthday as I had become accustomed to, and I know my ex-husband felt at home.

At the end of the service, like our church in Denver, they turned down the lights, and the missing windows took on a whole new appearance. They had candles in all the windows—somehow, I had missed that before, and the singing of "Silent Night" and all the candles glowing has stuck in my memory all these years as a very special Christmas Eve.

~

DENVER, COLORADO

Then after Rudolph and I married in 1973, I joined his church, St. Philip and St. James Episcopal church (lovingly known as St. PJs). His family traditionally went to Midnight Mass at their church—a brand new experience for me, which I adopted.

When we first married and were living in Denver, this night became a huge celebration. His mom made pancakes for dinner, a smaller meal with anticipation of a big dinner the next day. Sometimes we opened gifts on Christmas Eve, sometimes Christmas morning. But the big event Christmas Eve was Midnight Mass.

What an experience with all the candles lit, a Christmas tree up front, and the clergy in their beautiful robes. Cedar boughs draped the walls. The music sent chills over me, and then communion celebrating Jesus's birth with family and friends. The service ended with the lights lowered and the singing of "Silent Night." I wept at the sheer beauty of the evening.

Then the celebration began downstairs! The congregation put on a major potluck and all of Rudolph's high school friends returned, so it was a reunion! What fun! Often, over the years we lived in Denver, we never got home before 2:00 a.m.

~

TRINIDAD WITH MOM AND THEN ALSO DAD

After my ex-husband and I divorced in 1980, my love of the Christmas Eve Midnight Mass continued, and I went whenever I could. When I was in Branson with my parents, I discovered that the Lutheran Church in Trinidad did a Midnight service, not mass. So, Mom and I started going.

We left Branson around 10:00 p.m., so we faced the danger of wildlife on the highway. We filled the fifty-mile trip to Trinidad with stories and laughter, and I always drove watching the barrow ditches for whatever might pop out.

When we arrived, we received a warm welcome. We didn't go to that church, but we knew many of the congregants. Even though it wasn't a Mass, the service was beautiful and fulfilled my need for a Christmas Eve Midnight service to honor the birth of Christ.

On the way home, we stopped at a filling station on the west edge of Trinidad for a coffee for the late-night drive home. Again, we kept alert for wildlife and never had an accident.

After a couple years, Dad offered to join us. Being an agnostic and not a church-goer, Mom and I didn't initially invite him to join us. But watching us leave each year on this holiday night, leaving him home alone and then hearing how much we enjoyed it, he wanted to come. And he thoroughly enjoyed the late-night outing with us, being with us and seeing friends at the service.

DES MOINES, NEW MEXICO

After Dad died in 1996, I attended several Christmas Eve services at Mom's Methodist church in Des Moines, New Mexico. We met my cousin and her family there. Most of those services were in the early evening, so afterward, we visited with lifelong friends from the area. Even after Mom died in 2013, I continued going to her church on Christmas Eve with Lin.

OLD TOWN, ALBUQUERQUE, NEW MEXICO

In 2008, Mom and I ventured to Old Town Albuquerque on Christmas Eve after the early service at my church. We had trouble finding a parking space, so we parked in the Walgreen's parking lot on Rio Grande and Mountain—not a good idea since we could have gotten towed away, but we didn't.

Luminarias, as mentioned before, lined the walks as we headed toward the plaza. People overflowed everywhere. As we neared the corner of the San Felipe de Neri Catholic Church and the plaza, a live Nativity scene surprised us with animals and Mary and Joseph. Did they have a live baby Jesus out in the wintery cold? We didn't see one, but we heard rumors that there had been one there earlier in the evening. Captivated by the live scene, we lingered there a while, soaking in the familiar setting come alive.

After, we walked across the street to the plaza ablaze with luminarias, a spectacular sight. We joined the chorus of people walking through the maze of lights, enjoying their soft glow. After our leisure time there, we reluctantly headed home.

But I showed Mom one more New Mexico tradition on the drive home—luminarias around graves. We drove by a nearby cemetery, and once again the glow of the luminarias took over as we saw grave after grave encircled with the paper lights and families celebrating Christmas Eve with a missed loved one. What a memorable Christmas Eve, New Mexico-style!

~

TIJERAS, NEW MEXICO

During the pandemic, Lin and I attended Christmas Eve Mass at my church via Facebook Live, sitting in our front room at

5:30 p.m. What a treat that was! Even though we were at home, I dressed up in my Santa Claus dress, put on hose and makeup, and acted as if I was actually there.

A COUPLE YEARS AGO, my church added "La Posada," a Spanish tradition, to our Christmas Eve program. In a musical presentation, a cantata, Mary and Joseph go from house to house and are refused a place to stay by the neighbors until the last one. I loved the unique props they used. For each house, they had a simple paper door the neighbors held up and then swung away. Then the neighbor sang his refusal, to which Joseph responded in song, and then the holy couple moved on. The simplicity made it so easy to visualize the reality of the situation—no room!

~

Even to this day, Christmas Eve Midnight Mass is my favorite church service of the year. I love the festive colors, the candles, and the music, especially ending the service with dim lights, lit candle in my hands and "Silent Night."

CHAPTER TWENTY-THREE

ENJOY FOUR NEW MEXICO CHRISTMAS TRADITIONS!

A traditional New Mexico Christmas differs from the rest of the world with four amazing traditions: tamales, bisochitos, empanadas, and luminarias. The first three Mexican specialties add delicious flavor to any meal, and the last one lights up our towns!

TAMALES

"Tamales are a traditional Mexican dish made with a corn-based dough mixture that is filled with various meats or beans and cheese. Tamales are wrapped and cooked in corn husks or banana leaves, but they are removed from the husks before eating. Try them served with pico de gallo on top and a side of guacamole and rice."[1]

I'm lucky because I have a dear ninety-three-year-old friend in Branson, Colorado who usually gives us tamales when she makes them. Making tamales takes a lot of time, effort, and knowledge. I have never had the opportunity to assist my friend, but I would like to sometime.

Every year for Christmas, my husband's Costa Rican ex-wife gives us Costa Rican tamales, wrapped in banana leaves and some secret additions that are yummy! We wait for her phone call to let us know they're in the mail! Delicious!

When I grew up, someone in our small town made a delicacy: sweet tamales that had fruit inside instead of meat. Growing up, I had these more often than the meat-filled tamale.

When I went to Mexico as a young married woman in the 1970s, my husband and I ate dinner at a buffet featuring Mexican food. I saw a sign above a dish saying "tamale" and grabbed one, not reading closely, remembering the sweet tamales I had as a child. I choked and sputtered as I swallowed the first bit of the tamale, thinking it would be sweet, but it had meat inside! I almost spit it out but couldn't. So prepare yourself! There are two types: meat-filled or fruit-filled.

If you're interested in fixing your own, here's a YouTube video on how to do it:

https://www.youtube.com/watch?v=gkQh3UUjezs

~

BISOCHITOS

Bisochitos became the official state cookie of New Mexico in 1989, and if you've had one, you will know why! This rich cookie melts in your mouth as you savor its cinnamon and captivating anise flavor.

"There are several variations of this recipe, but the flavors are the same . . . cinnamon sugar and anise. Some people use shortening instead of lard. Some people use anise oil instead of the real thing. Some people use brandy or rum instead of white wine."[2]

Albuquerque's own Pastian's Bakery tops my list for bisochitos: absolutely scrumptious! We square dance with Sheri Pastian, the owner, and normally we have the pleasure of eating Pastian's bisochitos at many holiday dances.

Visit Pastian's Bakery for the best in Albuquerque: https://www.pastiansbakery.com/biscochitos

~

EMPANADAS

A New Mexico favorite, empanadas, can be both a sweet treat for dessert or a savory meal. It looks like a half moon pie filled with delicious fruit fillings or meat. I like mine sweet. As a dessert or a treat with a cup of coffee, an empanada adds to the holiday festivities.

Here's a recipe for a sweet empanada:
https://www.muydelish.com/sweet-empanadas/

LUMINARIAS

Albuquerque, and any town in New Mexico and the Southwest, lights up at Christmas like the rest of the world, but traditionally we enjoy a different type of lights, luminarias.

"The glowing brown sacks that adorn Albuquerque walkways, churches, and homes each holiday season are called luminarias and date back more than three hundred years. The New Mexican tradition began when the Spanish villages along the Rio Grande displayed the unique and easy-to-make Christmas lanterns, called luminarias, to welcome the Christ child into the world. A traditional luminaria is a brown paper bag, which has been folded at the top, filled with a couple cups of sand and a votive candle."[3]

In New Mexico, starting December 1st, we see big displays in many stores of stacks of paper sacks and votive candles to make our own luminarias. Then all that's needed is sand to put in the sack's bottom to stabilize the bag.

If you don't want to do it yourself, Boy Scout troops offer

great deals and deliver luminarias by the dozens to your home before the holiday rush.

Traditionally we put luminarias out on Christmas Eve. In fact, there's a great luminaria tour around the Old Town area and surrounding neighborhoods in Albuquerque, New Mexico. I love the golden glow created by the luminarias all lined up in a row.

In 2008, my mom and I drove down to Old Town on Christmas Eve and saw luminarias lining the streets around the plaza and San Felipe de Neri Catholic Church. The church also provided a live Nativity scene. Here's a chance to visit this inspiring church: https://sanfelipedeneri.org/

Also, many New Mexicans line the graves of their loved ones with luminarias on Christmas Eve, so our graveyards become a celebration of light on this night.

I didn't grow up with this tradition in Colorado, and I will never forget the first time I saw the lineup of paper bags before they were lit and wondered what they were. Then, when lit, they took my breath away.

Tamales spice up a meal. Bisochitos end any holiday meal with the delicious anise and cinnamon flavor! Empanadas stand as the main dish or dessert—your choice! Luminarias light our path! Yes, a New Mexico Christmas enjoys these four local traditions.

I'm sure I've missed a favorite New Mexico Christmas tradition of yours? Let me know if I did. What are your local unusual holiday traditions?

---

1. https://tastesbetterfromscratch.com/mexican-tamales/
2. http://www.tortillasandhoney.com/2012/04/biscochitos-new-mexicos-official-state.html
3. https://www.visitalbuquerque.org/about-abq/culture-heritage/holiday-traditions/luminarias/

CHAPTER
TWENTY-FOUR
I HAD NO IDEA!

In 2010, Lin and I celebrated Christmas with Mom and my elderly Aunt Willie in snowy Branson, Colorado. Over the past couple of months, I had seen signs of Lin and my new romantic relationship deepening, and we had shared several conversations about a future, so our being together on the holiday made it extra special.

When we turned off the highway into the driveway, I chuckled to myself. There in the window where Mom put her Christmas tree every year stood a retro three-foot silver tree Aunt Willie had given her. She decorated it simply with small purple balls, celebrating her favorite color. Yes, she had her small tree now!

We arrived in the early afternoon of Christmas Eve and opened our Advent gifts that day. Remember the Advent tradition Mom started before I went into treatment? This year I included Lin and Aunt Willie in that pre-Christmas gift-giving Mom and I had shared for many years. I bought Lin and Aunt Willie some silly children's Christmas activity booklets, and they chuckled but held them close.

As we sat and visited on Christmas Eve, we decided to stay

home because of the snow. Then the power went off. Yes, it had snowed a couple days before, but not that night. I have no idea why we lost electricity. Country living sometimes has no explanations for such outages. First, we grabbed Mom's trusty kerosene lamps from the top shelf of the buffet. She kept them there for just this reason. The soft glow immediately reminded me of many childhood nights when the electricity went off, especially in summer thunderstorms.

Then we improvised the evening's entertainment by playing games from Lin and Aunt Willie's children's Christmas activity booklets. These booklets saved our night with lots of laughter.

Also, Lin beguiled us with his humor. He's a great joke teller! What could have been a disaster of an evening turned into a memorable time filled with laughter and crazy humor.

Christmas morning, Mom and I dressed alike in silly Christmas PJs I bought us—red candy cane tops and green pants. Aunt Willie sat in the recliner with a smile on her face, enjoying being included. Mom sat on the wicker loveseat across from Lin and me on the sofa. We opened our presents with much fanfare and frivolity. It was so right. Aunt Willie's presence added to the holiday spirit.

After clearing out the wrinkled Christmas paper and scattered bows, Lin cleared his throat and said some introductory words. Mom must have realized what was coming, but I didn't. She grabbed her camera.

When he got down on one knee and said, "We've been talking about this for quite some time. Would you marry me?"

Shocked, words escaped me, so I nodded my head, "Yes," and both witnesses cheered!

Yes, we had talked about it, but had barriers in the way. I was the president of Single Square Dancers USA—and had agreed to a three-year commitment when I accepted in 2009: vice president one year, then president, and finally current past president, to help with the transition. So, I still had until Labor Day weekend in 2011 to fulfill my commitment.

Also, Lin's previous wife, Kathi, who was my best square dance girlfriend, passed away November 25, 2009. My relationship with Lin had grown within six months of her death, so we wanted to be discreet about the timing of our wedding and his and my loss of her.

Yes, I wanted to marry Lin with all my heart, and his choice of location for this special point in time still chokes me up. The two most important women in my life witnessed this life-changing event in my most favorite place on earth—my home in Branson, Colorado. And Mom, with her camera in hand caught the moment for us!

Lin proposed to me on Christmas Day, 2010 in Branson, Colorado

CHAPTER
TWENTY-FIVE
CHRISTMAS SHOPPING DURING THE PANDEMIC?

"Christmas doesn't come from a store, maybe Christmas perhaps means a little bit more . . ."

Dr. Seuss

December 13, 2020

Christmas shopping coronavirus-style: has it been different for you? In New Mexico, we have restrictions limiting the number of people in a store, so if I go shopping, I have to wait in the queue outside in the cold. I have to be near people who could have the virus, and so far, my husband, Lin, and I have been spared. So, for me, the answer is simple—stay home and shop online! Here's a few places I visited: Amazon, Fanatics, Home Depot, Snapfish, and Shutterfly.

Over the last few years, I've bought many gifts online, whether for my husband, my brother, or the rest of my family, so I'm not new to this concept. One holiday tradition I've loved is going to Old Town Albuquerque for regional southwest gifts. I won't be doing that this year.

For this year's Christmas shopping, I've ordered ninety-nine percent online. I bought one gift while at Walmart this week.

When thinking about past Christmas gifts, I love making them and have done it for years, whether it was a hand-knitted garment or a photo gift. This year I've had to cancel my favorite gift I've given my family for twenty-three years—a family calendar featuring photos from the previous year.

A couple years after my dad died, one of my team teachers, Rebecca Betzen, reached out to my mom and put together a calendar filled with a variety of pictures from my childhood to my graduation dinner for my master's degree! Several pictures highlighted favorite places on our family ranch. Those pictures ignited fond memories as my mom and I flipped through the pages, and I needed that. The gift thrilled me so much that I decided to do the same thing for my own family the next year. The recipient list grew over the years. And it's a tradition I continued until the pandemic. We weren't together in 2020, so I have no pictures to highlight.

Sample of Horner Calendar, 2012

Each year I highlight whoever had a special event that year, like graduations or weddings. If a family member died the previous year, I featured him or her on the cover. I also featured our family ranch on the cover of several calendars, like the one above. My second cousin married in England in 2017, and Lin and I attended, with me taking lots of pictures. Her new husband said, "I bet we make the calendar next year!" And they did—front cover!

Over the years, these calendars have become keepsakes, logging the key events of each year.

My joy came when my family members opened this gift and leafed through the pages, laughing at certain pictures and making heartfelt remarks. These calendars have become a historic family document of our year together.

So, Christmas shopping did change slightly in 2020—especially the gift-giving part and not being able to see my family's faces when they opened the calendar—but I've stayed focused on the joy and celebration of this precious holiday and shopped online, staying safe through the holidays.[1]

---

1. Larada Horner-Miller, *Coronavirus Reflections: Bitter or Better?* (2021): 215-219.

CHAPTER TWENTY-SIX

CHRISTMAS 2020 WITH CHARLES DICKENS

"I will honor Christmas in my heart, and try to keep it all the year . . ."

Charles Dickens

December 20, 2020

Every year around Christmas, my husband, Lin, and I watch Charles Dickens's *A Christmas Carol*, a tradition we continued this year.

I know the story by heart. I studied Charles Dickens as an English major. I taught it to my sixth-grade literature class each year. We've watched it each year together, and our visit to Dickens's house in London in 2017 made it so much more real.

Ebenezer Scrooge, the story's central character, is full of a "Bah, humbug" attitude, focused on monetary rewards and negativity since the death in childbirth of his sister, Fan. This horrible event reflected Scrooge's own life story because his mother died in childbirth with him. The two deaths doubled his heartache, and he turned his back on his nephew, Fred. His heartache enlarged!

During this past year, I have witnessed similar darkness and horrible attitudes toward others, people refusing to think of others and wear a mask, affronting someone for wearing one or ridiculing me on Facebook for my stance on the subject. The pandemic brought out the worst in some people, likening them to Scrooge. I could almost hear "Bah, humbug" hidden in their responses.

Scrooge receives a visit from his former business partner, Jacob Marley, on Christmas Eve. Marley warns Scrooge of what's coming: visits from three spirits: the Spirits of Christmas Past, Present, and Yet to Come, who force Scrooge to face the shallow life he had lived since his sister's death.

In the story, Dickens poses Tiny Tim Cratchit, the crippled son of Bob who worked for Scrooge, as the opposite attitude. His positive response, "God bless us, everyone," and his personality totally contradict Scrooge's.

I try to embody Tiny Tim's attitude rather than Scrooge.

Over the last few months, we've repeatedly heard the mandate, "Stay at home," especially as we neared the Thanksgiving and Christmas holidays. The CDC feared families would gather for these precious holidays like normal and make them super-spreaders.

We had the choice, and continuing the conservative mindset we've embraced since the onset of the pandemic, Lin and I stayed home! We both have some health issues. He is eighty, and I am sixty-seven, so we enjoyed our traditions, our decorations, and connections with people through Zoom, YouTube Live, and the internet. Many others embraced the Tiny Tim mindset across this land and did the same.

Even though we made the choice to stay home, did this "stay at home" order affect my Christmas plans? In some ways, yes, it did; in some, no!

As I reflected on Dickens's three spirits, it catapulted me into remembering my wonderful Christmas past, delighting in my Christmas present with its celebrations and fun, and musing about Christmas Yet to Come, hopefully a return to a more normal time.

CHRISTMAS PAST

Year after year, my family got together at our family home in Branson, Colorado. The attendees changed over the years. As a child, we celebrated there with Dad's side of the family: grandparents, cousins, aunts, and uncles. These get-togethers were massive! I traveled there often in my adulthood with Mom and Dad hosting Mom's parents, aunts and uncles, cousins, and me.

Before my mom and Aunt Willie died, my niece and one of my cousins joined us a couple years, with their respective families.

Round table in Branson, Colorado where we gather around at Christmas

My niece hadn't spent much time on the ranch since she and her family had lived far away for her adult life, so we made frequent trips out there, familiarizing them with where it was and looking for wildlife. We all packed into the Bronco, then jumped out at our favorite spots on the ranch. With binoculars in hand, we scoured the canyons for wildlife: deer, elk, or maybe a bear. Once we thought we saw a mountain lion, at least, his tail, but we weren't sure!

Throughout all the years, we ate delicious meals, played lots of games around the round table, laughed, and shared gifts. We caught up with each other's lives, updating all with our own personal stories—a memorable time.

Over the years, our family had its moments where we all didn't get along, but the people faced the adverse effects, offered forgiveness, and we stayed connected.

Lin and me on Christmas Eve, 2020

CHRISTMAS PRESENT

Leading up to Christmas 2020, I have several Zoom parties with friends all over the world scheduled. I can't wait to see everyone's faces and celebrate with them through technology.

On Christmas Eve, Lin and I plan on attending a virtual Christmas Eve service streamed online by my church, Hope in the Desert Episcopal Church, in Albuquerque. For the first time this year, I actually dressed up and put on makeup, trying to keep some of my normal Christmas traditions.

Then on the actual day, Lin and I will celebrate a memorable quiet Christmas here at home alone in the east mountains above Albuquerque because we strongly agree with all the suggestions the CDC has issued about holiday gatherings. We will play Cribbage, reminiscing about our favorite childhood Christmases so long ago and also our precious Christmases together, and open gifts and celebrate our lives together. In the evening, we will watch one of the many Christmas movies we watch each year, like *White Christmas* or

Christmas in Connecticut. We'll laugh at the same familiar places and cry at our favorite heart-wrenching spots, too. It will be good because we have accepted the change we have to do to keep everyone in our family safe.

CHRISTMAS YET TO COME

I trust that next year we will again gather in Branson, sit around the table and play games with loved ones, and tell our tales of this time apart. We will visit the ranch we all love, looking for wildlife and reminiscing about all those special places we love. Dad and Mom continue to be central characters we talk about regularly.

And I will relish next year more than ever because of the loss of time together this year! Two great-nieces will have graduated high school; another one moved to Ohio. After this year, I will value my familial relationships more because of the stark lack of time with dear ones in 2020.

~

As you can see, family and storytelling weave their way through all of my three Christmas descriptions.

A Christmas Carol reflected Charles Dickens's life. Because his father was imprisoned for debt, his life changed drastically, and his writing highlighted the brutal changes in his life.

This story has strong implications for 2020: redemption and change. Scrooge spent the majority of his life in the darkness of negativity but became willing to change after he was forced to see the light that was always there. People today have the same opportunity for a similar transformation.

Can we collectively embrace Dickens's lessons from *A Christmas Carol*?

Not being able to spend quality time with our loved ones during the holidays is difficult, but it's possible to find alternative ways to deal with the restrictions currently necessary in order to keep the public safe. If you've battled the mandates, could you change from "Bah, humbug" to a more Tiny Tim attitude?

If you've railed about how the coronavirus caused cancelations of everything you hold dear this year, like your favorite square dance festival, could you say a quiet prayer for forgiveness and then pray for the families who lost someone to the horrible virus, a much more serious loss than mine?

If you've put yourself in the center of this drama called life in 2020 and been negative and selfish, could you bow your head and honor the healthcare workers who have placed their lives on the line for many every day selflessly?

If your family doesn't agree at all about the whole topic of the coronavirus, could you put aside your differences for the holidays and embrace the lifelong love that binds you together?

Yes, change is possible. Redemption is possible, but the

process requires awareness, acceptance, and action. The action is in the doing!

Can we take a breath and learn from Ebenezer Scrooge this Christmas? Not a negative "Bah, humbug" anymore, but Tiny Tim's glorious redemptive, "God bless us, everyone!"

December 27, 2020

So much is different in 2020! I hope that Christmas Yet to Come will proceed as I'd like, but for now, all I can do is focus on the present holiday, which has turned out to be blessed, even if it's been a different type of celebration. I had the pleasure of spending Christmas with Lin, who makes any holiday special with his positive attitude and hilarious sense of humor!

No matter what's going on in the world at Christmas, Jesus is the reason for the season any year, but I especially focused on Him this year. Because I had extra time, I spent more time contemplating this special holiday and its importance to me—the magic of the Nativity and the Christ child.

Usually I'm rushed, splintered, and frantic. This year, I took the time to concentrate on Jesus's birth and its importance in my life. I hope you did the same![1]

---

1. Larada Horner-Miller, *Coronavirus Reflections: Bitter or Better?* (2021): 221-229.

SCRIPTURE – LUKE 2:15-16

Luke 2:15-16 *When the angels went away from them into heaven,*

the shepherds said to one another, "Let us go over to Bethlehem and see this thing that has happened, which the Lord has made known to us."

And they went with haste and found Mary and Joseph, and the baby lying in a manger.

CHAPTER TWENTY-SEVEN

IS A NATIVITY SET IMPORTANT?

My Stained Glass Nativity

Nativity sets, trees, lights—what's your favorite Christmas decoration? Mine is my Nativity set collection that I feature with white lights on a buffet in my home. I want to share why I think it's an important part of my Christmas decorations.

The Nativity is what Christmas is about—Jesus's birth is the centerpiece with Mary and Joseph by his side. Three Wise Men bring their gifts of frankincense, gold, and myrrh. Shepherds kneel close to the Christ child in humble adoration. And an Angel stands near Jesus, glorifying his birth.

I have a fun collection of Nativity sets I've gathered over the years I'd like to share with you.

My Mobile Nativity Set

The oldest one I have is a plastercraft mobile I made in the 70s that we hang each year. I love the childlike figures that represent all the key players in the Nativity. Once I'd painted the figures, my ex-husband fashioned a piece of metal into a circle and punched holes where I laced pieces of fishing line to hang each figure. Then I centered the Christ child in the middle and added Mary and Joseph near. Then a little lower, I added the Wise Men and the shepherds.

My Three Wisemen Candle Holders

I also made a set of three Wise Men candleholders made of plastercraft. I had them set up on the mantel one Christmas and a wreath fell off the wall above them and knocked two of them off, injuring them slightly. But I've kept them and loved them every year.

My Tonala Blue Pottery Nativity Set

In my early travels to Mexico in the 70s, I noticed some beautiful blue pottery and bought a cup, saucer, and a plate of it. On another trip, I bought a beautiful pitcher. I found out on the internet this pottery is called Tonala blue pottery. Any time I went to Mexico, this pottery drew me to it. In the 80s, I bought a fourteen-piece Nativity set of this blue pottery. It's become the centerpiece in my collection every year. From an older set, I add some animals to fill it out.

I remember bringing that set home in a carry-on bag. Carefully, I wrapped each piece and worked hard to make sure nothing broke. They arrived safe and in one piece and have stayed unscathed.

Slowly over the years, I've added to my collection. I have a Native American set, a music box my brother and sister-in-law gave me, a Peruvian candleholder, and a small happy kids' set.

Music Box Nativity Set

Peruvian Candleholder

In 2020, I picked up a small set in Spain that looks very Gaudí!

Gaudí! Nativity Set

Native American Nativity Set

WHY DO I gather multi-ethnic Nativity sets? Jesus was a dark-skinned Middle Eastern man, yet many people only see him as they are—whatever the color of their skin! His nationality doesn't matter; therefore, He can be a Native American, a Mexican, a Middle Easterner, or an American!

I'll end with one more Nativity set—our outside set I inherited from my parents. I love looking out our kitchen window and seeing it lit up every night on our patio.

My Parent's Outside Nativity Set

My dad loved putting it up every Christmas on their porch and lighting it up.

Here's one of my favorite Christmas sayings: "Jesus is the reason for the season." That's why I set up my collection each year—to honor who this holiday is about!

Do you put up a Nativity set? What do you think?

CHAPTER
TWENTY-EIGHT
WHY A BABY?

As I prepared for Christmas one year, a thought came to me: "Why a baby?" It rolled around and around for days. I don't just accept the pat story I've heard year after year. I like to go deeper—see it from a different perspective. So, let's go back in time, to a special moment that changed the world.

A newborn baby coos and breathes a heavy sigh, feeling safe and warm. Mary rolls over and lays her arm around the baby to make sure he's okay. Joseph stirs because of Mary's movement. After a long trip and the eventful night of birth, the trio is deeply connected.

Tranquil animals surround these three in this stable in the little town of Bethlehem. A jersey cow moos softly and adjusts a hind leg that's cramped. A donkey brays and twitches an ear, its lazy eyes slowly closing to rest! Sheep move like shadows around the enclosure, chewing the scattered hay and enjoying the warmth generated by the other animals and humans. The peaceful mixture of sounds in that manger echoes through the centuries.

A baby—why did God decide to come to earth as a defenseless, dependent baby two-thousand-plus years ago?

The answer is easy: the allure of a baby is magical, especially a newborn. Just watch children and adults alike swarm to a newborn, the face of innocence and joy, and wonder at another miracle. Yes, a baby attracts most everyone to its side, and that's what God wanted.

So, this Christmas, make sure you take the time to really connect with the baby Jesus in that stable. Look into His eyes, touch His small round hands, and marvel that you are staring at the face of God!

Several years ago, I wrote the following short story, and it certainly connects during the Christmas season. Enjoy!

I Found My Answer

She looks so familiar; I've seen her before. I know she has the answer to the question that's been haunting me for months. All I have to do is get her alone and ask my question—my one big important question. But whenever I get close enough to her to ask, my parents throw their arms up to guard the baby and scream, "Be careful! She's fragile. You could hurt her."

I know why they're so paranoid. I heard Mom whispering to Dad about an accident at a neighbor's house where a toddler tried to care for a newborn baby and injured her. But I wouldn't do that!

I am so excited. You see, she's new. They just brought her home from the hospital yesterday. Her name is Ann. I'm Laurie, her three-year-old sister. I wasn't that excited about her when she was in my mom's tummy, but since I've seen her face, I know she's got the answer. If only they'd let me near her, alone!

I try to outfox them—one time after another, I almost get to her—to whisper my question in her ear. Something deep inside me recognizes her and her spirit. But my parents always stop me. It's frustrating. What am I to do?

I have to get to her before she forgets, like I have. Or have I? I have a vague recollection. Cloudy images float through my mind at times that are a part of the answer, but I know she knows for sure!

My deep desire for the answer only increases; my tactics change, but nothing seems to work. They're set on protecting her from me, and I'm equally set on getting to her for the answer.

I stand by my mom as she holds her—that beautiful cherub face ready to tell me, but I know I need to wait until Mom isn't there so I can get near Ann. She gets upset when I try to get really close to Ann. And to get my answer, I have to whisper right in Ann's ear. Then hopefully I'll hear her response, because I know the answer will come softly, in words no adult can recognize. I think I can still understand, though. That I haven't outgrown the language. Before, I knew it: the language, the words, the answer. I've heard some of her sounds, and they sound vaguely familiar—

otherworldly, my world. I need little time, only minutes, but we need to be alone and quiet.

As weeks unfold, I don't give up, but my plans have changed. I stop the outright method; I wait and watch for the opportune time, and my patience finally pays off.

At six weeks old, Ann is baptized in our church. Mom and Dad hold her, and I stand nearby, eye-level with the baptismal font. I love the water and all the excitement. Ann doesn't cry when the water runs down her face. Boy, I would now! The priest says words I don't understand, but he has a faintly familiar face too. Maybe he could answer my question, but his words baffle me.

Afterwards, my parents throw a big party at our house, inviting family and friends to show off their new child. This proves to be the distraction I need.

The guests all "ooh" and "ah" over her and bring me gifts too so I won't feel left out. I'm not worried about gifts or sibling rivalry or stuff like that—I'm on a mission. My folks think I'm jealous of Ann, that I want to hurt her, but that's not true at all. If only I could explain it to them.

Mom has lots of delicious food and drink. Glasses tinkle, and it's a celebration. They enjoy good, lighthearted conversation with family and friends. For the first time since Ann arrived, my parents relax about me bothering my baby sister. The party atmosphere distracts them, so I'm on the move.

Startled back to reality, Mom asks my grandma, "Where's Laurie?" Everyone starts the search for me, but my time had come a few moments earlier when, quietly, I slipped out of the living room, up the stairs, and into my baby sister's room. She was sleeping, but that's okay. I know she'll still answer.

I pull a chair over to her crib and crawl up into it,

careful not to hurt her. Quietly, I lie down next to her and begin whispering my question into her ear—

"Tell me—what does God look like? I've been here for three long years, and I've almost forgotten."

A knowing smile crosses Ann's lips, and her answer came through. "He looks like me," I hear. I knew it! That's why she looked so familiar! Something inside me knew all along. Every time I've seen a baby in the last three years, I've gotten the urge to ask that question. I felt drawn to the newborns, but no one ever let me close enough to one before. Having a baby in my home made the asking easy—after I got past Mom and Dad.

That answer quieted my questioning spirit, and I was peaceful at last. At that moment, she reconnected me with my God. Hopefully, I could hold on to this truth for a few more years.

Little did I know my Aunt Janey was sitting in a rocking chair in the corner of the room and had heard the entire conversation (my side only because she can't hear babies.) My question touched her heart deeply.

She didn't move or try to stop me. I fell asleep beside my sister, finally at peace, and that's where my parents found me—resting after my quest had ended. I had found my answer.

What does the face of God look like to you?

CHAPTER

TWENTY-NINE

DO YOU KNOW MARY? DO YOU KNOW JOSEPH?

Sitting at a Starbucks with my laptop in early December and Christmas in the air, I pondered if I really knew Mary and Joseph. As I sat, drinking my peppermint latte, I googled the Christmas story, a handy tool because I didn't have my Bible with me. I knew the familiar names, the story, but who were they? This is what I came up with!

~

A YOUNG JEWISH girl humbly accepted a visit from God's angel Gabriel and puzzled over his message that she would be the mother of the Messiah. At first, she couldn't fathom the idea. The Jewish world had been waiting centuries for His coming. The prophets had predicted it. She was a teenager and single. What a shock!

Being single, Mary questioned Gabriel about how she could give birth to a child. Patiently, Gabriel explained the mystery. Her humble response echoes through the ages: "I am the Lord's servant." Her answer was "Yes!"

Mary's song, in response, recorded in Luke 1:46-55, is a celebration of her commitment to do God's will. Read it out loud and celebrate her obedience.

Imagine what those nine months after an angel's visit were like. Some sort of marriage happened. Blindsided by Mary's preposterous explanation of her pregnancy, Joseph protected Mary during this time. Somehow, he knew this child she carried was special. Pregnancy outside of marriage during this time was scandalous!

As her time neared, they had to rush to Bethlehem from their hometown of Nazareth. Caesar Augustus ordered a census, which required people to return to their hometowns to be registered. and Joseph belonged to the house and lineage of David, so they went to Bethlehem to register Mary.

Nine months pregnant, Mary faced a 160-kilometer trip. Did she walk part of the way and ride a donkey the rest? How long did it take? In today's world, it's a two and a half hour trip, but theirs had to take hours, maybe days.

Each mounting step jarred this pregnant woman. As she neared Bethlehem, the birth pangs hit. Did her water break before or after they found the manger? Was the pain unbearable? As they moved from inn to inn, Joseph realized there was no place to stay—the census had overloaded the small Jewish city. What to do?

Thinking creatively, he found an empty stable and tied his tired donkey up. Gently, he lifted Mary off its back and nestled her in a soft bed of hay. The time had arrived. He delivered his child, the Son of God, alone in their makeshift home.

Mary trusted his judgment and knew that they would be okay. Her screams echoed through the hills. Joseph wiped the sweat from her brow, praying for God's guidance. One last scream, and a new soft sound filled the quiet night—the cry of a newborn baby. God directed him on how to cut the umbilical cord and tend to Mary's needs.

Joseph wrapped his newborn son in cloths they had brought with them and placed him in the manger. Cattle and donkeys nibbled on the hay that surrounded our Savior. His heart burst with pride—a son to carry on his carpentry business, his own son—but wait! This was God's son! What did that mean for Joseph and Jesus?

Mary's eyes focused on the baby, Jesus—her baby. Tears welled up in her eyes as her heart burst with joy! Her baby boy was here! She savored the serenity of the moment. Then the quiet stable changed as the twosome noticed an angel appear. The trumpet blast from the angel announcing the birth of Jesus shattered the silence. The cows and donkeys in the stable stirred and joined the chorus of angels in celebrating this birth. Shepherds drifted in the door with their sheep and bowed to the newborn King. They shed tears of joy in the promise's fulfillment! They moved aside but lingered as three wise men laid gifts— gold, frankincense, and myrrh—at the feet of this amazing baby. This mixture of Jew and Gentile surprised Mary and Joseph.

Mary and Joseph looked at each other in amazement and

smiled—it was true! The message from Gabriel nine months ago was true! They were now the parents of the Son of God!

THESE ARE my thoughts about a familiar story.

Have you ever thought about what happened that night so long ago in Bethlehem? I challenge you to do so this Christmas.

CHAPTER THIRTY

THE DAY AFTER CHRISTMAS—NOW WHAT?

The day after Christmas is here! Santa and most parents need a vacation. Now, what? As a child, I focused on playing with my new toys on this day. As an adult, what do I do? How do I conjure up the sheer joy the new toy brought every year as an adult?

~

HERE'S what we did one year:

LOOKING BACK

Looking back on my Christmas preparations, I created a calendar for a family gift. I wrote, designed, and published our annual Christmas newsletter. Then, I sent cards to friends far and near. During Advent, I took part in a group that read Richard Rohr's *Preparing for Christmas*, then we shared comments and remarks on WhatsApp because we had an international group taking part. What a rewarding group that was!

CHRISTMAS EVE

I had an errand day in Albuquerque, getting a prescription and some groceries. At 5:00 p.m., Lin and I virtually attended the Christmas Eve service at Hope in the Desert Episcopal Church. It started with "La Posada," a Mexican tradition of the pregnant Mary and Joseph going house to house and being denied any lodging. The last home welcomes them in. In its simplicity, it was beautiful.

After the service, we ate Costa Rican tamales from Lin's ex-wife. While we ate, we watched two traditional Christmas movies: *Scrooge* and *It's a Beautiful Life.* Then we watched a contemporary movie on Amazon Prime with a strong Christian message.

Lin and Me on Christmas Eve, 2021

CHRISTMAS DAY

On Christmas morning, we opened our gifts and ate blueberry empanadas from Pastian's Bakery. After that, we played two Cribbage games. Lin worked hard so he wouldn't skunk me on Christmas Day—what a loving man! We ate a late lunch—honey-baked ham, cheesy cheddar potatoes, asparagus, and applesauce. Later, we enjoyed pecan pie. Lin added eggnog ice cream.

From that point on, Lin watched the two football games scheduled for Christmas day. That's always shocking to me to have football at Christmas. I made a big batch of popcorn balls

—my favorite Christmas goodies. I neglected to get my traditional baking in this year, so this ended up being a great time to do it.

DURING THE DAY, we both called friends we knew were having a hard time this holiday. One lost her dad this year and was alone. The other recently lost her husband of fifty-three years. We called another long-time friend in an assisted living facility. Sharing those calls made our day! We are so blessed to have each other!

~

THE DAY AFTER CHRISTMAS

So, here we are the day after Christmas. Usually, mega commercials for after-Christmas sales dominate our TV viewing. I've seen none! Probably because shoppers picked over Christmas items weeks ago. I went to our grocery store last week, and hardly anything was available. Is this because of shortages or supply chain irregularities due to the pandemic? Unusual, no matter what. Mom used to love to go to these sales, looking for great buys!

I've always enjoyed this day. As a child, I familiarized myself with whatever new toy I received. As a high school student, we stayed up late each night and watched Johnny Carson and, later, Jay Leno on "The Tonight Show."

Later, I savored the time with Dad and Mom, with stories and trips to the ranch. After my niece moved to Texas, she often arrived in Branson the day after Christmas. With her and her family in tow, we looked forward to a few days of loud games at the round table, with laughter and stories and trips to the ranch looking for wildlife.

~

EXTENDED Christmas Season

For me, just because Christmas Day is behind me, the Christmas season isn't over. My church celebrates the "Twelve Days of Christmas," which ends at Epiphany, "a Christian festival held on January 6 in honor of the coming of the three kings to the infant Jesus Christ."[1]

So, I keep wearing my Christmas outfits and happily enjoy extending the holiday. We don't take our tree down until after Epiphany. I love this longer holiday season.

Many people have a big letdown on the day after

Christmas—holiday expectations not met, memories of better times haunt people by the changes today, etc. You fill in the blank with whatever weighs on you today.

This year, on this day after Christmas, try something different. Call someone who may need cheering up, family or friend. Ask a family member about what Christmas was like when they were children, listen and ask questions to draw out more specifics. Dust off your stack of games and have a marathon game day. Tonight, make up some hot chocolate, or grab your coat and hat to look at Christmas decorations in your area.

Finally, the day after Christmas has arrived—enjoy it!

WHAT DO you do the day after Christmas? Do you do anything traditional? If so, what? If not, add one of my suggestions or get creative!

---

1. https://www.merriam-webster.com/dictionary/epiphany

CHAPTER

THIRTY-ONE

EPIPHANY 2021: LIGHT & DARKNESS COLLIDE

On Epiphany 2021, January 6th became a day in USA history. Light and darkness collided with few even aware of that fact. Most years, this ecclesiastical day goes unnoticed except for those who celebrate it in the liturgical calendar. I will never forget this year.

So, what is Epiphany to me, as an Episcopalian? ". . . the

church celebrates the Feast of the Epiphany, which marks the end of the twelve days of Christmas each year on January 6. Epiphany is a Greek word meaning 'manifestation' or 'appearing.' At the Feast of the Epiphany, we celebrate Jesus being made manifest or appearing as Christ."[1]

The Episcopal church says: Epiphany is ". . . the manifestation of Christ to the peoples of the earth. The day was called 'The Feast of Lights.'"[2]

"The gifts seem quite strange to give to a baby, but Christians believe that they had the following meanings:

• "Gold: is associated with Kings and Christians believe that Jesus is the King of Kings.

• Frankincense: is sometimes used in worship in Churches and showed that people would worship Jesus. Frankincense (also sometimes called olibanum) is a resin from trees in the genus Boswellia.

• Myrrh: is a perfume that is put on dead bodies to make them smell nice; Christian believe that it showed that Jesus would suffer and die."[3]

Normally, I have mixed feelings with the arrival of

Epiphany because it marks the end of Christmas, and I love the Christmas season and everything about it. I love Epiphany, though, because of its focus: Jesus, the light of the world. Epiphany is a celebratory time.

In 2021, I dreaded this day for weeks ahead of time. I knew it coincided with the certification of the results of the 2020 election by Congress in the United States. Also, I knew protesters planned an event in Washington, D.C.

When the day came, initially I forgot it was January 6. I did my normal routine: my Quiet Time reading and writing in the morning, rousing Cribbage games with Lin, my husband, during breakfast, and normal stuff. At 11:00 a.m., I had a Zoom meeting with my marketing agent and ten other authors.

After finishing that peaceful, supportive meeting, I headed downstairs. Lin rushed in the door, returning from a trip to Walmart. He had listened to a news station on Sirius, and said, "Turn on the TV. They're storming the Capitol."

I did; we ate lunch, trying to digest the horrific activity before our eyes. The protesters had breached our Capitol. I sat glued to the TV for the rest of the afternoon and early evening. Image after image exploded on the screen of these lawless invaders looting the Capitol. This Epiphany, darkness raised its ugly head.

As I watched, I cried! I posted my despair on Facebook and received massive support and one dissenter. What a dark day in our history! I realized that day stood as a turning point in my life for acceptance of the lies perpetuated over the last two months about the election and the results. It had been brewing for four years, so I set boundaries on Facebook with supporters of this sedition.

As the afternoon dimmed into night, I remembered Father Dan Tuton, the priest at my Episcopal church, had scheduled a Zoom Epiphany Service, and I had planned to attend. Should I? What fresh development would I miss? My hours-long vigil had worn me out. I needed to refocus on God and love and light.

Earlier in the day, I had shared with Lin that I planned to attend this service, and he joined me. I want to thank Father Dan Tuton and Hope in the Desert Episcopal Church[4] for a peaceful reflective Epiphany service during such a turbulent day. He read Matthew 2:1-12, recounting the Magi's visit to the Messiah. Then he read Henry Van Dyke's, *The Story of the Other Wise Man*.

How I needed that time bathed in the glory of Epiphany! God works in mysterious ways, for sure. Right before we took an intermission at the mid-point in Van Dyke's story, a dear friend messaged me with a personal prayer request. I shared it with the group, and we prayed right then. I knew they would because my church is a healing community. Whew! My God, in the middle of chaos!

The images from that infamous day whirl around in my mind still. Because I'm a historian and record keeper, I downloaded several images of the looters, the terrorists, the destruction. Why would I do that? Possibly, I would use them in a blog, but no! I do not want to give them any more notoriety. Instead, I want to provide a respite from the chaos.

Let's focus on the light, the Christ child who lights up my

life. Father Dan helped me refocus from a sad day to a commemoration of three wise men (or more or less. No one knows for sure) who traveled a long distance to confirm the birth of the Messiah, as described in Matthew, who witnessed the beginning of His life.

As we continued reading Van Dyke's story, *The Story of the Other Wise Man*, he revealed another possible wise man, Artaban, who touched my heart with his willingness to give his gifts intended for the Messiah to those in need. In doing that, he missed the Magi's finding of the Christ child but had a serendipitous meeting with Jesus later.

So, this sad day ended on a positive note, with a celebration of the Magi honoring the Christ child and the giving spirit of Artaban. I felt God's light and love emanating from this Scripture, this tale, and this service.

How can we refocus when darkness seems to prevail? How can we identify the goodness of our country (USA) and its people?

---

1. https://episcopalchurch.org/files/bi010613half.pdf
2. https://episcopalchurch.org/library/glossary/epiphany
3. https://www.whychristmas.com/story/wisemen
4. https://www.hopepiscopal.org/

CHAPTER THIRTY-TWO

OUR NAMES DIDN'T MATTER; OUR MISSION DID! AN EPIPHANY STORY

The Christmas story includes three Wise Men, but through the ages, we know little about them. My curiosity had been piqued when Father Dan Tuton, my priest, introduced me to the book, *The Story of the Other Wise Man.* My imagination took off, and here's a story I wrote on this trio:

~

"I'M NOT JEWISH, and I'm not going!" This powerful statement from one of our members shocked me, and I stared wide-eyed at my other two like-minded companions. To me—to us three—this would be the biggest event since I joined this auspicious group of seers or astrologers. We love the stars and study them in this group.

That star in the East had haunted me the last few days, luring me in that direction. But we had to talk to the group and see what the consensus was, so I curbed my rash desire to just flee East with no plan nor explanation.

The majority of our group filed out in silence, sneering at our idea of seeking this new King of the Jews and his birth. "Why?" they repeated throughout the meeting. Men of wisdom had studied Judaism and some of its prophecies and identified this bright star in the East as a cosmic event but lacked specifics. They needed more facts, but it still left the three of us astounded to see them walk out.

"Well, I guess it's just us three going, then."

We didn't let their apathy affect our anticipation. We prepared to travel to Jerusalem to talk to Herod, a Roman-appointed King of Judea. For sure, he would know what all this meant.

We gathered our travel gear and lined up our camels for the long trek. We talked to our families, warning them we did not know when we would return. Our trio had to represent our country there with gifts and the customary protocol.

What gifts should we bring? After much discussion about what was suitable for a King of this caliber, we decided on three priceless gifts: gold, frankincense, and myrrh.

Gold

Frankincense

Myrrh

The plan was to leave in the morning, but the bright star in the East kept urging me on. Nervous and anxious, I slept little that night, rose early, and stood ready to go by my camel when the other two arrived.

We talked a little on the trip and kept our eyes glued on the star. It hovered over a specific place, and we knew, somehow, our mission was ordained.

Arriving in Jerusalem, my heartbeat increased. We were close. Our talk with Herod confused me, though. Our observation about the birth of a King shocked him, but why should it? He was a Roman-appointed King of Judea and knew nothing of the Jewish prophecy. His advisors scurried around and gathered the information we needed. Our wise council did not have the specific prophecy—they did.

Herod's council told us Jewish Holy books predicted the Messiah would be born in Bethlehem in Judea. I knew little about the Jewish religion and wondered why Herod hadn't noticed the bright star and put two and two together, like we did.

We didn't linger there because the three of us felt an urgency to see this King. The little over nine-kilometer trip from Jerusalem to Bethlehem took us two hours, but our pace increased as we neared our destination.

The brilliantly lit star hung over a place of meager means. My camel's rumbling growl seemed to expect something. The other two camels joined in. We dismounted, dusted our cloaks off, and grabbed the gifts we brought.

Surprisingly, Joseph met us at the door like he was expecting us. He ushered us into his home, a manger where cattle mooed and donkeys brayed. I felt a divine presence as I saw a beautiful young Jewish mother cuddling her newborn baby son in her arms. An aura of love surrounded the duo, as if the star above had anointed them.

Then I fell to my knees as I saw His face. I knew deeply that this child held power like I had never experienced. Looking for my two friends, I wanted them to witness this miracle. Both had fallen to their knees, too, faces aglow with wonder and mystery.

Solemnly, we presented our three gifts at the feet of Mary and her baby. Joseph talked quietly to us, asking where we had come from. He seemed in awe of us, foreigners to his land.

Meekly, I stepped closer and ventured to touch the baby's cheek—sweet and precious. I looked into his open eyes and saw the face of God and knew I'd never be the same. His attraction drew my friends to his side, and they, too, wanted to touch him. In her serene manner, Mary nodded her head. They touched his cheek, too, and I saw a visible change in their faces as they witnessed him.

None of us wanted to leave, but I felt we had stayed long enough to be polite—any longer could be disrespectful. When we left, we camped near Bethlehem, thinking we'd retrace our steps back to Jerusalem. Herod had requested we report back to him about our find.

After our experience, we sat around the campfire, warming ourselves, mulling over our full day. The world had just changed, and we knew we had played a part in it. Finally, the fire burned down, and we snuggled into our bedrolls.

The last thing I remember before falling to sleep is the glow of the embers and the glow in my heart.

During the night, I saw a warning in my dreams—*don't go back to Herod. He's dangerous and means harm to this new King.*

The next morning, I shared this frightful dream with my friends, and we traveled home by a different route.

We could not get home quickly enough. We convened our group and reported our findings. The mild reception concerned me, but I knew that my mission on earth was set—God had come to earth through this baby, the King of the Jews, and he had opened the door to the entire Gentile world through our simple obedience.

I confided in my wife and parents about this miracle, and their lukewarm response surprised me. But it didn't alter what I saw and experienced.

You will never hear my name mentioned in any holy book or literature—it doesn't matter. What matters is that my two friends and I traveled the distance, witnessed the birth of the Christ child, and spread the news to our world!

THAT'S my fictional take on the Wise Men. In our observation of Epiphany, we celebrate the coming of the Wise Men to the Christ child. We believe that the Wise Men's visit to the Christ child opened access to the Gentile world and the entire world.

What are your thoughts?

CHAPTER THIRTY-THREE

LANGUAGES & "MERRY CHRISTMAS"

I love languages and was a Spanish teacher at the middle school level for fourteen years! In December 2022, Lin and I returned from a cruise touring Spain and Italy. It ended up in Portugal. Holiday decorations appeared at the beginning of December, so I decided I wanted to learn how each country said Merry Christmas. I added a couple of new "Merry Christmas" greetings to my repertoire. Merry Christmas in Italian, Spanish, and Portuguese, and how they say it in the Philippines! What a welcoming worldwide greeting!

In each country, I practiced as much as possible and received lots of smiles, giggles, and responses when I said Merry Christmas in their languages. I greeted shop clerks, workers at the airport, and anyone I could! Practice was important for retention—the teacher came out in me.

The first language (other than English) that I learned how to say "Merry Christmas" in was Spanish many, many years ago—Feliz Navidad! And one of my favorite Christmas songs is Jose Feliciano's "Feliz Navidad."

HOWEVER, IT'S PRONOUNCED DIFFERENTLY HERE IN THE UNITED STATES AND MEXICO THAN IN SPAIN:

https://www.youtube.com/watch?v=8iA5tNhLT-M

AND HERE'S HOW MERRY CHRISTMAS IN SPANISH IS PRONOUNCED IN SPAIN:

https://youtu.be/7wWnoutO7bg

Notice the difference: they pronounce the "z" and "d" sounds as "th" in Spain.

HERE'S HOW TO SAY MERRY CHRISTMAS IN ITALIAN:

https://www.youtube.com/watch?v=UjJ6r8QoRvE

~

AND HOW TO SAY MERRY CHRISTMAS IN PORTUGAL:

https://youtu.be/tX7NfFRj258

Notice the similarity to the Spanish pronunciation and spelling of the first word.

~

ONE OF OUR servers on the cruise ship also shared with me how to say Merry Christmas in the Philippines, so here it is. It sounds musical!

https://youtu.be/aT_57ZK1sXk

~

THIS HOLIDAY TRIP ignited my interest in languages, so I'd like to end with a wonderful video showing how to say Merry Christmas in several languages:

https://youtu.be/fAF0o9ls598

~

THROUGHOUT OUR TRAVELS, I reveled in this worldwide holiday celebrating the birth of Jesus Christ! I so enjoyed the decorations in the different countries: twinkling lights, Santa

Claus, and Nativities that mirrored ours in the States. More than anything, though, I loved learning these greetings.

Can you say Merry Christmas in different languages? Check out these videos I've listed and share them with your family and friends.

CONCLUSION

I love Christmas and all my memories of this special day. Yes, it's only one day a year, but celebrating the entire season leading up to it, and the days afterward, fulfills me as an adult —and as an eternal child.

These memories lift me up as I grow older. Each time a

specific event comes up, I rush for my computer to capture the thought and the feeling. I hope that enchantment never dies.

It's a magical time, filled with choices. I choose to keep it Christ-centered yet celebratory, conjuring up childhood images and excitement.

My favorite carols fill the air; I sing along out loud if I'm alone driving in the car or silently with others. My collection of Christmas CDs overflows. I also have albums from my teen years. One particular song, "I'll be Home for Christmas" with Floyd Cramer's beautiful piano music catapults me to time alone as a teenager.

Mom and Dad had made a quick trip to town for last minute shopping. My brother hadn't come home yet from basketball practice. With no one else home, I had turned all the lights out except the tree, turned on the record player with Floyd playing that song, and felt a nostalgia overcome me. I looked to the future and felt the draw of home at Christmas. Anticipating my few years left at home and all it represented, at that moment, I lay on the sofa and cried with that song.

Today whenever I hear that song, no matter who sings or plays it, it magically takes me back to that moment in time.

That eternal child need never die—we must keep him/her alive to celebrate Christmas another year!

Merry Christmas from me to you!

Merry Christmas to all, old and young! And as Tiny Tim said, "God bless us everyone!"

APPENDIX A

Popcorn Balls Recipe

Elaine Kennedy

- 1 1/2 c. sugar
- 1/2 c. Karo syrup
- 1/2 c. water
- 1 stick oleo
- 1 tsp. salt
- Vanilla

Cook until it forms a soft ball in cold water. Add vanilla (and food coloring). Pour over popped corn. Wet hand (with cold water) and form balls.[1]

---

1. Folsom Garden Club. *Garden of Recipes,* (1972): 69.

SOME OF MY CHRISTMAS FAVORITES

CHRISTMAS READINGS:

- ***A Christmas Carol***, Charles Dickens
- ***The Best Christmas Pageant Ever***, Barbara Robinson

- ***The Gift of the Magic***, O. Henry
- ***Skipping Christmas,*** John Grisham
- ***"Twas the Night Before Christmas,"*** Clement C. Moore
- ***"Papa Noel,"*** Floyd Beard - Audio
- ***The Christmas Train***, David Baldacci
- ***How the Grinch Stole Christmas,*** Theodor "Dr. Seuss" Geisel

CHRISTMAS MOVIES:

- ***White Christmas***
- ***Holiday Inn***
- ***Miracle on 34th Street***
- ***It's a Wonderful Life***
- ***A Christmas Carol***
- ***Christmas in Connecticut***
- ***A Christmas Story***
- ***The Bishop's Wife***

- *The Polar Express*
- *Dr. Seuss's The Grinch*
- *A Charlie Brown Christmas*
- *Rudolph, the Red-Nosed Reindeer*
- *Love Actually*
- *Home Alone*
- *National Lampoon Christmas Vacation*
- *The Santa Clause*
- *The Man Who Invented Christmas*
- *Elf*

IF YOU ENJOYED THIS BOOK, THEN . . .

If you enjoyed these Christmas stories and poems,
Please leave a review on Amazon and/or Goodreads

and

visit my website:
https://www.LaradasBooks.com

JOIN ME!

Want to keep up on the latest in my writing world? Discounts, insights to my writing and more!
Join my team for a monthly newsletter and receive a free e-book gift:
https://mailchi.mp/76ef0e8040d4/free-tumbleweed

About the Author

Larada Horner-Miller is an award-winning poet, essayist, blogger and accomplished multi-genre author who holds a bachelor's degree in English, with a minor in Spanish and a master of education degree in Integrating Technology into the Classroom. She is the accomplished author of five award-winning biographies, historical fiction, memoir, and poetry works plus three self-published cookbooks.

Her sixth book, *Coronavirus Reflections: Bitter or Better?*, is available in paperback and four e-book formats. This book became a #1 best-seller in five e-book categories on Amazon and won the 2022 New Mexico/Arizona Book Award for the Mind, Body and Spirit category.

Larada Horner-Miller

Larada offers the reader the opportunity to look back at 2020 and the global pandemic through her prose and poetry through reading, then reflecting and responding. She addresses all the emotions she felt during this overwhelming time and leads the reader through to a self-access: bitter or better?

Her fifth book is the authorized biography of world-renown square dance caller Marshall "Flip" Flippo. *Just Another Square Dance Caller: Authorized Biography of*

Marshall Flippo is available now in hardback, paperback and four e-book formats. *Just Another Square Dance Caller* won two awards: Book Excellence Awards Finalist and Silver award for eLit. Book Awards.

Another book of hers, *A Time to Grow Up: A Daughter's Grief Memoir* has won many awards including being a 2018 Book Excellence Awards Finalist in the Memoir category at the New Mexico-Arizona Book Awards and a 2018 Independent Press Distinguished Favorites Award in the Memoir category. Horner-Miller has also been a past national presenter at the Women Writing the West Conference and is currently the creator of Memoir Workshops for others who want to share their family's legacies through words.

Larada and her husband, Lin, enjoy being nestled in the mountains above Albuquerque, New Mexico, near the village of Tijeras. When not writing books, this passionate, energetic, and enthusiastic woman loves to spend time kicking up her heels at square dancing gatherings, traveling, knitting, and reading.

As co-manager of her family's southeastern Colorado ranch, she enjoys spending time exploring her family's historic ranch and reminiscing with her brother and his children about their mom and dad.

Larada also enjoys her twenty-year-old cat, Jesse, a silver-tip Siamese. He has feline diabetes, so she has to give him insulin twice a day. She rescued him in 2009, so she's enjoyed him for fourteen years. Her mom said he was one of God's angels because he came to Larada during a difficult time in her life.

To learn more, visit https://laradasbooks.com/

facebook.com/Larada.author
twitter.com/laradah
instagram.com/larada_hm

Also by Larada Horner-Miller

OTHER BOOKS:

- *This Tumbleweed Landed*
- *When Will Papa Get Home?*
- *Let Me Tell You a Story*
- *A Time to Grow Up: A Daughter's Grief Memoir*
- *Just Another Square Dance Caller: Authorized Biography of Marshall Flippo*
- *Coronavirus Reflections: Bitter or Better?*

Enjoy my books in poetry and prose from my childhood, a story I fictionalized, how my granddad put our ranch together during the depression, losing my parents, the one and only Marshall Flippo and my reaction to the coronavirus pandemic!

~

AUDIOBOOK:

- *Let Me Tell You a Story*

COOKBOOK SERIES

- *From Grannie's Kitchen* - ***Pies, Cakes & Christmas Candy***, *Volume 1*
- *From Grannie's Kitchen* - **Beverages, Cookies, Meats, Vegetables, Mis. & Records of a Rancher's Wife**, *Volume 2*
- *From Grannie's Kitchen* - **Casseroles, Mexican Dishes, Relish, Sandwiches, Salads & Desserts**, *Volume 3*

FUTURE BOOKS BY LARADA HORNER-MILLER

- Four Poetry Book Series - Poetry
- I Said Yes! You Can Too!: How I Learned to Write a Biography - Writing Help
- Eyewitness to Healing: How One Life Changed So Many - Novel

Made in the USA
Coppell, TX
30 September 2023